British Warships & Auxiliaries

HMS Albion

THE ROYAL NAVY

The Cold War officially ended with the fall of the Soviet Block in 1989. For western politicians this was manna from heaven as it meant they could slash military budgets across the board. This is exactly what has happened in the UK over the last thirty years causing Former Chief of the Defence Staff, Admiral Lord Boyce to publicly state: '*Our number of frigates and destroyers are anorexic, and this has been exacerbated by the Type 45 problem. We embarked upon an eight-ship, Type 26 frigate building programme in 2017, but the first ship, Glasgow, won't be commissioned until 2027.*"

The United Kingdom takes a decade to build one ship, China builds a frigate of comparable firepower in months. Furthermore, China builds many, many more hulls than Britain can afford to purchase.

That the Royal Navy is just a shadow of its former glory is well-known amongst naval commentators, it is perhaps less well-known to the general public who neither know nor probably care about the issue. In the last year, their focus has squarely been focused on fighting a global pandemic and keeping themselves and their families safe. But it is just as important to keep our nation's borders, lines of communication and resupply safe and secure from all threats be they foreign military powers, soft warfare in the form of cyber and internet attack, or combating the worst effects of COVID-19 and future viruses that could yet again overwhelm us. The world in 2020 was brought to its knees by something we cannot see, smell, touch, or taste, but it is lethal, the millions who sadly died prematurely from contracting it are testimony to this appalling fact.

Britain's armed forces are not solely for making war, they are for securing the peace too. Members of the armed forces, the Royal Navy included, worked on the frontline in the battle against COVID-19 at testing centres and they brought with them the logistical and organisational skills that only properly trained and funded military personnel can.

In 2021, with the pandemic far from over, the world is on a far from secure footing. The threats are real and growing be they from a resurgent Russia intent of regaining past military glories and territory with landgrabs being the order of the day in Ukraine and the Crimean-peninsula as well as threats to the Baltic states.

There is an economic threat to our survival from around the globe and with the United Kingdom no longer a member of the European Union, does our independence put us at greater risk or, conversely, does it give us a different perspective?

Then there is the undeniable threat posed by the exponential military and economic growth of China and its bully-boy tactics over its illegal claims to vast stetches of the South China Seas. Into this arena, the Royal Navy in 2021, sent the new Carrier Strike Group headed by HMS QUEEN ELIZABETH, onboard F-35B Lightning II Joint Strike Fighters from Britain, and the United States Marine Corps. With the aircraft carrier are a strong escort of British, Dutch, and American warships. All to stare down the Chinese Dragon and reassert British interests in Asia Pacific.

Indeed, the narrative of Prime Minister Boris Johnson's address to Parliament in announcing the core themes of March's Integrated Strategic Review was to shift Britain's focus from Europe and the Northern Atlantic towards Asia Pacific. This is the very same area of the world that former US Secretary of the Navy, Kenneth J. Braithwaith feared the most during his short tenure in post during the last days of the Trump Administration.

He said of China: *"We have moved into a new era of great power competition facing up to great challenges around the globe that are unprecedented, truly unprecedented. What I mean by that is, never has the concept of democracy, of freedom, the things that we hold near and dear, the things you and I grew up with, ever been under the kind of pressure and future threats and challenges... that concept of democracy is under immense pressure today. I've seen it with my own eyes."*

The West views China and its communist leaders with a high level of suspicion and wariness, not least because of their handling of the COVID-19 crisis and for the suppression of free speech in Hong Kong. What the Chinese leadership thinks of the West, only the Chinese leadership knows.

Queen Elizabeth-class aircraft carriers
2021 will see QUEEN ELIZABETH deploy at the centre of the UK's Carrier Strike Group to the Indo Pacific region. This will mark the first British aircraft carrier deployment anywhere in over a decade since the premature withdrawal of ARK ROYAL. ELIZABETH will be supported by two type 45 destroyers, DEFENDER and DIAMOND, two Type 23 frigates, KENT and RICHMOND, an Astute-class submarine, RFA FORT VICTORIA and HNLMS EVERTSEN and the USS THE SULLIVANS as her escort group. To take four escorts out of the severely denuded Royal Navy total of just nineteen, will inevitably cause shortage elsewhere; but Great Britain and her carriers will need to put on a good show to the world in the summer of 2021. The deployment will also set several firsts; the first time the US Marines of VMFA-211 will be part of the air group; the first time Merlin Mk2 AEW Crowsnest will be integrated into the fleet greatly increasing the Carrier Strike Group's detection range. This will be a distinct advantage in the troubled waters of the South China Sea where QUEEN ELIZABETH is intentionally being sent to practise Freedom of Navigation exercises against strong competition from the Chinese Government.

Sistership PRINCE OF WALES will, in 2021, have returned to sea following multi-million repairs following a significant leak that damaged areas of the ship.

Amphibious

Following the sale of the Royal Navy's last Landing Platform Helicopter OCEAN to the Brazilian Navy, the Royal Navy now only operates the two Landing Platform Docks, ALBION and BULWARK. Perennially, these two large manpower intensive vessels are touted as the next sacrificial lambs to the slaughter on the altar of defence economies. Prior to the announcement of the 2021 Integrated Defence and Security Review there were, again, suggestions that they would be decommissioned early. The Defence Review, however, retained them until their planned out of service dates of 2033 and 2034 respectively.

The review also stated that the current system of one operational LPD (currently ALBION) whilst the other is in reserve or deep refit should continue. BULWARK will re-emerge from her current Extended Readiness in 2023. ALBION will then replace her for the next three years in reserve.

LSD(A)

The LSD(A)s are extremely useful and versatile vessels. There are three ships in service, LYME BAY, CARDIGAN BAY and MOUNTS BAY - a fourth, LARGS BAY was sold to Australia. These ships are heavily used with one permanently deployed to the Persian Gulf acting as mother ship to the minesweeper force there. Following the Integrated Defence Review, one of the three LSD(A)s will be converted in a £50 million refit to serve as a

HMS Albion

dedicated vessel for the Royal Marines. This will further erode the availability of the class for taskings elsewhere. There was no word from Government regarding additional orders for follow-on ships of this class in the Defence Review.

The Royal Marines themselves are to see an expanded role being deployed aboard active forward deployed warships. Future Commando Force will receive £200 million of extra funding to transform the service. Certainly, when QUEEN ELIZABETH sails to the Far East a complement of RM Commandos will form part of her crew.

Destroyers
The well-publicised propulsion systems deficiencies of the six Daring-class Type 45 destroyers are now, finally, being addressed. The Propulsion Improvement Programme (PIP) or Project Napier is well-underway. DAUNTLESS is the first of the class to see the upgrade with the installation of three, rather than the current two MTU diesel generators. DAUNTLESS, as of February 2021, was in the final stages of the upgrade. Sister ship DARING is the next ship to receive the refit. In fact, DARING has been effectively out of service for the last five years either serving as a harbour training ship or since 2019 been in refit.

The Type 45 destroyers, whilst excellent air defence ships, continue to lack any significant strike capability, notably lacking anti-land strike weapons such as Tomahawk. Furthermore, two out of the six ships are lacking anti-ship missiles such as Harpoon. The Type 45s were designed to have these weapons, but they are rarely fitted on the grounds of cost. The Defence Review made no mention of addressing this deficiency.

Incidentally, the anti-ship Harpoon missile is fast approaching obsolescence due to a lack of data link and radar terminal guidance systems. The missiles fitted to Type 23 frigates and some (not all) Type 45 destroyers was planned to be out of service in 2018, although its new out-of-service date has been put back to 2023. The Royal Navy lacks any great punch with its anti-ship missile inventory when compared with the latest Russian and Chinese hypersonic, extreme range missiles. The new missiles can travel at speeds of up to 7 times the speed of sound and cover ranges measured in hundreds, if not thousands, of miles. The Harpoon is around Mach 1 and has a range of under 100 miles.

The Royal Navy is not alone in this situation as the US Navy is in a similar situation of racing to catch up with the threat. Many missile manufacturers, notably the Israeli IAI has recently offered to supply the Royal Navy with their Sea Serpent anti-ship missile. Whether the Royal Navy can purchase 'off the shelf' will ultimately come down to budgetary considerations.

In the meantime, after 2023, anti-ship attack by Type 23 and Type 45s will be the sole domain of Sea Venom armed Wildcat helicopters. Sea Venom is designed to attack targets not larger than a corvette, anything bigger will surely pose a significant problem.

Frigates

If you were to believe the media frenzy around orders for new frigates you might be allowed to think that 2021/22 will be a bonanza year for Royal Navy escorts. Well, you'd only be half right. Yes, the Government has committed to building the Type 26 and Type 31e frigates and even surprised many naval commentators with word of a further follow-on design, the Type 32. Yet British warship construction is incredibly, ponderously slow. It takes around 20 years for a new design to emerge as a fully-fledged, manned, and operational warship at sea. The construction of GLASGOW, first of class of the Type 26 frigates will have been a whole decade from ordering to delivery.

During, this embarrassingly long time, older Type 23 frigates will have been withdrawn leaving the fleet even weaker in strength than before the words of the 2021 Integrated Defence Review. However, under current plans, whilst the number of escorts will dip as low as 19, it will by the early 2030s, rise once again to 24 escort vessels with the steady drumbeat delivery of Type 26 and Type 31e vessels into service allowing the worn-out venerable Type 23s to be retired from service.

The Defence Review also announced the withdrawal from service of MONTROSE and MONMOUTH. They will be decommissioned four and five years earlier than planned, respectively. However, the Government did announce plans to build the escort force up to 24 over time with the new Type 26 and Type 31e frigates entering service from 2027, progressively replacing the Type 23s. Under current plans eight Type 26 frigates will be built and five Type 31e and five Type 32s in due course.

The out-of-service dates for the remaining Type 23s will remain as planned: ARGYLL 2023, LANCASTER 2024, IRON DUKE 2025, WESTMINSTER 2028, NORTHUMBERLAND 2029, RICHMOND 2030, SOMERSET 2031, SUTHERLAND 2032, KENT 2033, PORTLAND 2034, ST ALBANS 2035.

Submarines

2021 saw the withdrawal of TRENCHANT, leaving TALENT and TRIUMPH of the legacy Trafalgar-class to soldier on past their scheduled out-of-service dates. Why? Because of serious problems in the construction and delivery of their successors, the Astute Class. To be fair, the Astutes are some of the most complicated and sophisticated man-made moving objects on the planet, and to design and build such machines is an awesome undertaking. Since last year's edition of BWA, AUDACIOUS has been delivered to the Royal Navy, and ANSON was rolled out of the construction hall at BAE Submarine Solutions at Barrow-in-Furness in mid-April 2021. AGAMEMNON and AGINCOURT are still under construction.

The MOD is, understandably, tight lipped about talking publicly about the Astute Class delays and it seems inevitable that knock-on delays in deliveries of the last submarines of the Class will occur. The Government, meanwhile, in the Integrated Defence and Security Review revealed that work on an Astute successor is well in hand. This will come as some relief to the management and workforce at BAE Submarine Solutions who will have a steady drumbeat of work on Astute, Dreadnought and Successor programmes for the next two decades to come.

HMS Medway

SSBNs

The Government has not waivered in its commitment to maintaining Britain's independent nuclear deterrent. They have increased the number of nuclear warheads available to the fleet. Of the Vanguards, their life extension programme continues. VANGUARD's refit has been delayed considerably due to unforeseen circumstances and is not expected to return to service until 2022. VICTORIOUS will take VANGUARD's place at Devonport in due course. This inevitably means that there are only two boats, VIGILANT and VENGEANCE, to maintain the UK's continuous-at-sea deterrent patrol that has been maintained since the first, RESOLUTION in June 1968.

The first and second Dreadnought-class SSBNs are currently under construction. Named DREADNOUGHT and VALIANT, they are considerably larger than the already vast Vanguard-class boats. The names of the other two planned submarines have been announced as WARSPITE and KING GEORGE VI, to honour the Queen's late father.

CROWN COPYRIGHT/MOD   **HMS Queen Elizabeth**

Submarine weapons

The Defence Review committed millions of pounds to developing superior Spearfish torpedoes alongside developing improved Stingray torpedoes. There was no word, however, of the UK's stockholding of Tomahawk cruise missiles. The UK Government doesn't usually comment on how many missiles are available, but it has been stated the policy is to not maintain more than 60. Each Astute-class submarine can carry up to 38 Tomahawks, which if deployed in one submarine would equal to more than 50 percent of the UK's entire stockholding.

Patrol boats

The construction and delivery of SPEY has seen the five-ship River II-class programme come to an end. These ships, designed for UK waters, have now, however, mostly been deployed abroad as 'colonial' type gunships in the Falklands, the Caribbean and Gibraltar, with others probably destined to be deployed to the Persian Gulf, Gulf of Guinea and even Asia. That the class can achieve this forward basing is admirable, but it does highlight the lack of any patrol vessels in British waters beyond the older, less capable River-class siblings, TYNE, MERSEY, and SEVERN.

This last trio of ships were originally to have been decommissioned but have been reprieved to serve the Fishery Protection/Border Protection role. With the United Kingdom leaving the EU at the beginning of 2021 this is a task that will increasingly become more important as European trawlers 'illegally' fish in UK territorial waters that were once EU waters. How long the River I-class will remain in service has not been confirmed.

The question of Fishery Protection is something that used to be addressed by minesweepers and minehunters, but the Hunts and Sandown-classes will quite rapidly be withdrawn from service with the planned introduction of automated drone minesweeping technologies. The introduction of autonomous systems is perhaps the greatest technological change that will affect the Royal Navy in the coming decade and comes with a £1 billion investment.

Another issue the withdrawal of smaller ships raises for the future of the Royal Navy is the lack of junior command opportunities. Junior officers highlighted for commanding ships get their first taste of command in small ships such as minehunters, but with their withdrawal (albeit on the grounds of cost and safety) where will they gain the experience of commanding a ship and crew?

Ocean Reconnaissance Vessel

The Government somewhat surprised those watching the announcement of the Defence Review when they said that a new 'multi-role ocean surveillance ship' will be added to the fleet. The protection of vital undersea communication cables and a replacement vessel for the soon-to-be retired SCOTT. The ship will enter service within three years and will be equipped with advanced sensors and remotely operated and autonomous undersea drones.

Conclusion

The Royal Navy is facing an interesting, challenging, and transformative time ahead. The service will see a drop, albeit temporary, in the number of available escorts but will by the mid-2030s, see a rise in the number of escorts to 24. There will be more opportunity to see the world as the Government pivots its global focus on the Far East and India and slightly shifts away from its current Eurocentric status.

There will be issues ahead for weaponry, particularly long-range strike missiles and the MARS Solid Support ship replacement programme, should, within five years, finally, see new ships delivered whether they are built in the United Kingdom or not. The Royal Marines will also experience a transformation into a swifter, more agile and lethal force, whilst the Silent Service will, hopefully, get a handle on the delivery schedule of new Astute-class submarines.

Further down the line, new classes of submarines, SSN successors, new Type 83 destroyers, and new Type 26, 31 and 32 frigates will come on stream, as will new innovative mine-warfare technologies.

First Sea Lord Admiral Tony Radakin said: *"The review is the most wide-ranging for a generation and it sets out the government's priorities for Defence. The Secretary of State wants us to respond better to the threats we face. We will. The Prime Minister wants us to be the foremost Navy in Europe. We will be. The White Ensign will fly in all the places where we are now, but also further afield and more persistently. All of us now have a new responsibility to deliver a global Navy for a global Britain."*

At the heart of the new Royal Navy, however, will remain the men and women who drive it forward, sustain it and represent the United Kingdom around the world in the finest traditions of the Senior Service.

Patrick Boniface
Naval Author & Editorial Correspondent Warship World
May 2021

SHIPS OF THE ROYAL NAVY
Pennant Numbers

Entries displayed in lighter typeface have yet to be completed

Royal Navy Submarines

HMS Astute

HMS Vengeance

SUBMARINES

VANGUARD CLASS

Ship	Pennant Number	Completion Date	Builder
VANGUARD	S28	1992	VSEL
VICTORIOUS	S29	1994	VSEL
VIGILANT	S30	1997	VSEL
VENGEANCE	S31	1999	VSEL

Displacement: 15,980 tonnes (submerged) **Dimensions:** 149.9m x 12.8m x 12m **Machinery:** 1 x Rolls-Royce PWR2 nuclear reactor; 2 GEC Turbines, 27,500 hp; single shaft; pump jet propulsor; two auxiliary retractable propulsion motors **Speed:** 25 + submerged **Armament:** 16 Tubes for Lockheed Trident 2 (D5) missiles, 4 Torpedo Tubes **Complement:** 135 (14 officers)

Notes: These four submarines are the second generation of Britain's Independent Nuclear Deterrent. Since 1994, when VANGUARD made her first deployment, this class have performed the silent and little reported role in total secrecy. Each submarine is armed with Trident 2 D5 missiles armed with independent nuclear re-entry vehicles. The number of these re-entry vehicles is being reassessed upwards following the publication of the 2021 Integrated Strategic Defence Review.

The submarines are based at Faslane in Scotland and each boat has two captains and two crews which means the duty crew are out while their opposite number are training or on leave. At least one of these submarines is always on patrol somewhere in the world, a second is training and a third is undergoing routine maintenance. The fourth is usually in deep long-term refit or refuelling at Plymouth.

In 2020 the Royal Navy allowed TV crews onboard VENGEANCE with presenter Rob Bell spending five-nights onboard. He was granted unprecedented access to life aboard what are known as Boomer Boats.

The Vanguard Class are all over 20 years old and will, in due course, be replaced in service by the new Dreadnought Class currently in build at BAE Systems Shipyard at Barrow-in-Furness. In the meantime, a life extension programme has been initiated to prolong the service careers of VIGILENT and VENGEANCE out to beyond 2028.

CROWN COPYRIGHT/MOD — **HMS Vanguard**

SUBMARINES
DREADNOUGHT CLASS

Ship	Pennant Number	Completion Date	Builder
DREADNOUGHT	-	-	*BAE Systems (Submarine)*
VALIANT	-	-	*BAE Systems (Submarine)*
WARSPITE	-	-	*BAE Systems (Submarine)*
KING GEORGE VI	-	-	*BAE Systems (Submarine)*

Displacement: 17,200 tonnes (submerged) **Dimensions:** 153.6m **Machinery:** 1 x Rolls-Royce PWR3 nuclear reactor; Turbo-electric drive, pump jet propulsor; single shaft **Speed:** -- **Armament:** 12 x ballistic missile tubes for 8-12 Lockheed Trident II D5 missiles, 4 x 21inch torpedo tubes for Spearfish heavyweight torpedoes **Complement:** 130

Notes: In May 2011, the Government announced the initial assessment phase for new submarines to replace the Vanguard-class submarines carrying Britain's Independent Nuclear Deterrent. The decision met with vehement objections from anti-nuclear campaigners and others who objected to the cost of the programme put at £31 billion. At the same time the Government placed orders for long lead time items for the submarines including the nuclear reactors to power them and the specialist high strength steel required to maintain deep diving capabilities.

Four years later after the Conservative Party's win at the 2015 elections, the Government committed to maintaining the deterrent with four so called 'Successor' submarines. This decision was put to a vote in Parliament on 18 July 2016 at which time it passed into law by 472 votes to 117.

As the only shipyard in the United Kingdom able to build complex submarines, BAE Systems was contracted to build the first submarine with construction of DREADNOUGHT, commencing on 6 October 2016. It is expected that she will enter service in 2028 in time to replace VANGUARD, which will by then be 30 years old. Construction on the second-in-class, VALIANT, commenced in September 2019.

The Dreadnought Class will have an intended service life longer than the current Vanguards at between 35 to 40 years and will be powered by a nuclear reactor that will not need to be refuelled throughout the operational lifetime of the submarine, greatly reducing maintenance, and running costs for the future fleet of four submarines. The missile tubes for the Trident missiles are the same as those being developed for the US Navy's Columbia-class of successor ballistic missile submarines.

The sensors aboard the submarines are expected to be state-of-the-art upon completion and boast items such as second-generation optronic masts instead of traditional periscopes. These masts will be constructed at Govan by Barr and Stroud who have been making submarine periscopes for almost one hundred years.

DREADNOUGHT and her sisters will be the largest submarines ever operated by the Royal Navy and the most powerful. They also feature separate compartments for male and female personnel, a first on RN submarines. Special lighting arrangements aboard will imitate the day and night on the surface thus making life underwater easier to adapt to for submariners.

The submarines will benefit from the installation of 'Fly-by-wire' technology equivalent to systems found on modern airliners. The Active Vehicle Control Management System will oversee all major aspects of the submarines manoeuvring including heading, pitch, depth, and buoyancy. The new system is being developed by BAE Systems Controls and Avionics at their site in Rochester in Kent and will use computers to supplement the work of 'planesmen' operating the submarines, in what is a very physically and mentally demanding role aboard.

CROWN COPYRIGHT/MOD

HMS Vengeance

HMS Artful

ASTUTE CLASS

Ship	Pennant Number	Completion Date	Builder
ASTUTE	S119	2007	BAE Systems (Submarine)
AMBUSH	S120	2012	BAE Systems (Submarine)
ARTFUL	S121	2015	BAE Systems (Submarine)
AUDACIOUS	S122	2018	BAE Systems (Submarine)
ANSON	S124	2021	BAE Systems (Submarine)
AGAMEMNON	*S123*	*2023*	*BAE Submarine Solutions*
AGINCOURT	*S125*	*2026*	*BAE Submarine Solutions*

Displacement: 7,400 tonnes (7,800 tonnes submerged) **Dimensions:** 97m x 11.2m x 9.5m **Machinery:** Rolls-Royce PWR2; 2 Alsthom Turbines, 27,500 hp; single shaft; pump jet propulsor; two motors for emergency drive; one auxiliary retractable propeller **Speed:** 29+ submerged **Armament:** 6 Torpedo Tubes; Spearfish torpedoes; Tomahawk cruise missiles for a payload of 38 weapons **Complement:** 110 (including 12 Officers)

Notes: This class of nuclear-powered submarine is the direct successor to the extremely successful Trafalgar-class vessels but were designed to incorporate a raft of new technologies and systems unheard of when the Trafalgars were in build.

The Astute Class are designed to fulfil a wide-range of strategic and tactical roles within the Royal Navy from anti-ship and anti-submarine warfare, surveillance and intelligence gathering to support of land forces and the delivery of long-range ordnance (Tomahawk cruise missiles) to targets deep within enemy territories. Each submarine has a dock down capability allowing divers to operate from the boat whilst it remains submerged

150t(75t+75t)

ANSON
BAE SYSTEMS

HMS Anson

and undetected. This is in addition to the Chalfont dry deck hangar which can be loaded and unloaded onto the back of the submarines for specialised swimmer teams for stand off insertion missions for specialist forces.

At the heart of the Astute-class submarines is the BAE Common Combat System (CCS) which was first fully tested aboard ARTFUL in February 2016. Essentially CCS is a computerised brain within the submarine that controls all its sensors in a similar way to a human nervous system interacts with its ears, eyes, and nose. The system can interpret sonar readings and coordinate appropriate attacks on enemy submarines accordingly. The system was introduced from build on AUDACIOUS and on all new build submarines after that, with retrofitting on older boats at scheduled refit dates.

AUDACIOUS was launched on 28 April 2017 and commenced sea trials in 2018. After that date however, the programme has slipped considerably due to 'emergent technical issues within the build programme which have required unplanned repair and rework to facilitate the submarine proceeding forward within the normal commissioning process'. As of January 2021, AUDACIOUS still has not become operational, although it is expected that she will soon become so. These delays have affected the schedule for the remainder of the class pushing it back several months.

On 21 April, BAE Systems rolled out ANSON at their site in Barrow-in-Furness, Cumbria. ANSON, the fifth of seven Astute-class submarines being built for the Royal Navy, entered the water for the very first time. She will now begin the next phase of her test and commissioning programme, before leaving Barrow for sea trials with the Navy in 2022.

Construction of the remaining two, AGAMEMNON and AGINCOURT, proceed with the latter's expected handover to be sometime in 2026. The construction programme for the class has seen some significant improvements since the first three vessels were launched. ASTUTE arrived in the fleet costing £3,356 billion, a 58% increase over the original planned cost. Boats five and six however will be delivered to the Royal Navy at a cost of £1.42 billion and £1.533 billion respectively.

These boats are the largest and most advanced attack submarines ever built for the Royal Navy. At a length of 97m, they can circumnavigate the globe submerged and produce their own oxygen and drinking water.

DANIEL FERRO

HMS Talent

TRAFALGAR CLASS

Ship	Pennant Number	Completion Date	Builder
TRENCHANT	S91	1988	Vickers
TALENT	S92	1990	Vickers
TRIUMPH	S93	1991	Vickers

Displacement: 4,500 tonnes (5,298 tonnes submerged) **Dimensions:** 85.4m x 9.8m x 9.5m **Machinery:** Rolls-Royce PWR1; 2 GEC Turbines, 15,000 hp; single shaft; pump jet propulsor; one motor for emergency drive - retractable propeller **Speed:** 30+ dived **Armament:** 5 Torpedo Tubes; Spearfish torpedoes; Tomahawk cruise missiles for a payload of 24 weapons **Complement:** 130

Notes: At the end of March 2021 TRENCHANT sailed into her home port of Plymouth for the very last time. Devonport Naval Base welcomed home the oldest submarine in the Royal Navy fleet proudly flying her paying off pennant. As she arrived at Plymouth Sound a number of her crew 'went up top' to line the casing. She will be de-commissioned later this year.

During her 35-years on patrol there have been many highlights of her service, two of which have been her ice-patrols. In 2016 the boat punched through the ice and emerged on the surface of the Arctic Ocean. This marked nearly a decade since a British boat had carried out this manoeuvre, re-generating the Submarine Service's under-ice capability.

In 2018 in the harsh environment of the North Pole she broke through the ice again in an exercise with the US Navy.

The remaining two Trafalgar-class submarines are the survivors of a class of seven nuclear attack submarines, and even this pair should, by rights, already have been removed from service, but delays in the Astute Class programme have meant that they have been retained in active service beyond their original out-of-service dates. The Trafalgar Class has, since the mid-1980s, been the backbone of the Royal Navy's Silent Service, but even in their autumn years the submarines still have a vital role to play in Britain's defence.

In early 2021 TALENT was used to test launch the latest variant of the heavyweight Spearfish Mod 1 torpedo during trials conducted near the Isle of Skye. She was also witnessed sporting sensors which have been described as 'sub sniffers' in the press. The non-acoustic detection system was fitted to TALENT's bow and fin and can detect tiny radiation signatures from the power plant of enemy submarines and tiny pressure differences in a body of water caused by the passage of a submerged boat.

TALENT is scheduled to leave service later in 2021. TRIUMPH's scheduled decommissioning remains dependent on the delivery of the latest Astute-class submarine into service.

HMS Trenchant

Royal Navy Warships

HMS Duncan

CROWN COPYRIGHT/MOD

HMS Queen Elizabeth

AIRCRAFT CARRIER
QUEEN ELIZABETH CLASS

Ship	Pennant Number	Completion Date	Builder
QUEEN ELIZABETH	R08	2017	Aircraft Carrier Alliance
PRINCE OF WALES	R09	2019	Aircraft Carrier Alliance

Displacement: 65,500 tonnes FL **Dimensions:** 282.9m x 38.8m x 11m **Machinery:** Integrated Full Electric Propulsion; 2 RR MT30 GT alternators, 93,870 hp (70 MW), 4 Wärtsilä DG, 53,064 hp (39.6 MW); 4 induction motors, 53,640 hp (40 MW); 2 shafts **Speed:** 26 knots **Armament:** 3 x Phalanx, 4 x 30mm **Aircraft:** Up to 36 x F-35B Lightning and 4 x Merlin ASaC (Crowsnest). Typical mix could be 12-24 F-35B and various helicopters which could include Merlin, Chinook, Wildcat and Apache **Complement:** 686 + 830 Air Group

Notes: These 65,000 tonnes aircraft carriers are the largest and most complex surface vessels ever designed, built, and operated by the Royal Navy. Each ship can accommodate all military helicopter types currently in the British armed forces (Navy, Army and Air Force) and F-35B Lightning II Joint Strike Fighters.

The UK reached a major milestone in December 2020 when it declared its Carrier Strike programme had achieved Initial Operating Capability following a series of multi-national exercises throughout 2020. This Joint Declaration paves the way for a successful inaugural operational deployment of the UK Carrier Strike Group alongside its allies. Following the successful completion of QUEEN ELIZABETH's participation in EXERCISE JOINT WARRIOR the aircraft carrier was equipped with a full load of weapons in her magazines ready for the deployment.

On 19 January 2021 British Defence Secretary Ben Wallace and his acting US counterpart Christopher C Miller co-signed the UK-US Declaration for the Carrier Strike Group 2021 deployment. In a move highlighting the growing interdependency of the two nations to work together on naval strike, the US Marine Corps will deploy a detachment of F-35B Lightning II strike aircraft from VMFA-21 'Wake Island Avengers' aboard the QUEEN ELIZABETH during her maiden Far East deployment in 2021. The US Navy also committed the Arleigh Burke-class guided missile destroyer USS THE SULLIVANS (DDG-68) to form part of the aircraft carrier's escort group. Ben Wallace MP went onto say: "This deployment embodies the strength of our bilateral ties and reflects the depth and breadth of this vital defence and security partnership."

QUEEN ELIZABETH will be at the centre of a powerful task group made up of the following warships: DIAMOND, DEFENDER, KENT, RICHMOND, RFA FORT VICTORIA , plus a Tide-class tanker and a nuclear attack submarine (a Trafalgar or Astute Class). The Group will also include USS THE SULLIVANS and the Dutch HNLMS EVERTSEN. Additional temporary additions from Australia, New Zealand, Malaysia, India, Singapore and Japan are expected as the ship journeys through South East Asia and the Pacific regions. For the deployment, the aircraft carrier will benefit from the addition to her airwing of the first Merlin Crowsnest helicopters capable of lifting the powerful Crowsnest aerial radar into the sky to give an enhanced airborne surveillance and control of the battlespace around the Carrier Group. The Merlins fitted with Crowsnest will work alongside the rest of the Merlins embarked in the warship but they will have the distinctive radar deployed in large 'bags' attached to the fuselage, which gives the helicopters their nickname of 'Baggers'.

Prime Minister Boris Johnson, in his statement to Parliament announcing the Integrated Defence Review, said that Great Britain's future focus would be placed squarely on the Indo-Pacific region and QUEEN ELIZABETH's much heralded deployment is a further extension of this philosophy. It has already been greeted with disdain in China as something of a colonial last gasp of Empire banner waving. The Chinese have also publicly stated that appropriate measures will be taken by the PLAN (Peoples Liberation Army Navy) to stop the Task Group from exercising in what China considers its territory, the disputed South China Seas. Britain and the United States, however, consider the area to be international waters and regularly exercise Freedom of Navigation passages through the area much to the chagrin of the Chinese.

HMS Prince of Wales

PRINCE OF WALES suffered a minor flooding incident in May 2020, which was followed by a much more significant flooding event in October the same year, that has required a considerable amount of time, effort, and £3.3 million to fix. Consequently, PRINCE OF WALES had, in the entirety of 2020, only been to sea for 30 days, compared to 115 for her sister ship. One of those times was in February 2020 for a successful port of call to her affiliated city of Liverpool.

The MoD plans to introduce PRINCE OF WALES as a second carrier and another squadron of F-35B jets between 2020 and 2026. This will allow the carriers to perform a range of roles, including acting as a helicopter carrier in an amphibious capacity. Nevertheless, the MoD is having second thoughts about this and working towards concentrating on carrier strike for both ships and not to pursue the amphibious role. It is anticipated that when she does return to the fleet she will test the class's ability to operate in the amphibious assault role previously undertaken by the dedicated helicopter assault carrier OCEAN, sold to the Brazilian Navy in 2018. Unlike the assault ships ALBION and BULWARK however, she cannot operate landing craft and will only be able to operate in the helicopter assault role. It is expected that the Merlin HC4 Commando variant will be operated by PRINCE OF WALES in this role.

During her time alongside in Portsmouth PRINCE OF WALES was, in July 2020, the host of an exhibition of future military drone technology during the Future Maritime Aviation Accelerator Day. Numerous prototype unmanned aerial vehicles were demonstrated. Early in 2021 the Ministry of Defence announced a RFI (Request for Information) to industry for proposals for a catapult launch system for possible use aboard QUEEN ELIZABETH and PRINCE OF WALES, primarily for use with emergent UAV technologies. This comes as the Royal Navy seeks to develop and invest in the latest technology, bringing new, world-beating equipment to the frontline quicker.

HMS Prince of Wales

HMS Albion

LANDING PLATFORM DOCK
ALBION CLASS

Ship	Pennant Number	Completion Date	Builder
ALBION	L14	2003	BAE Systems
BULWARK	L15	2004	BAE Systems

Displacement: 18,797 tonnes FL, 21,500 tonnes (flooded) **Dimensions** 176m x 28.9m x 7.1m **Machinery:** Diesel-electric; 2 Wärtsilä Vasa 32E DG, 17,000 hp (12.5 MW); 2 Wärtsilä Vasa 32LNE DG, 4,216 hp (3.1 MW); 2 motors; 2 shafts; 1 bow thruster **Speed:** 18 knots **Armament:** 2 x CIWS, 2 x 20mm guns (single) **Complement:** 325 Military Lift 303 troops, with an overload capacity of a further 405

Notes: These highly versatile vessels provide the Royal Navy with its amphibious punch and were designed with the function of landing Royal Marines ashore by air and by sea. They also have extensive command and control facilities and can operate as flagships for operations and major deployments. Each ship has deck capacity for up to six Army Challenger main battle tanks or around 30 armoured all-terrain vehicles. A floodable well dock aft can accommodate four LCU Mk10 utility landing craft, while four smaller LCVP Mk5B landing craft are carried on davits. Both have a large flight deck capable of receiving all British and most Allied helicopter types currently in service, but neither have hangar facilities. The flight deck is arranged with two landing spots for simultaneous operation of two RAF Chinook helicopters. It is Royal Navy policy to have one of these vessels operational while the other is retained in reserve or refit. In 2017 ALBION re-emerged since being laid up since 2012 and assumed the role of Fleet Flagship, subsequently passed onto QUEEN ELIZABETH in 2020. BULWARK is currently slowly regenerating at Devonport and is expected to replace her sister ship in 2023. ALBION and BULWARK have out-of-service dates of 2033 and 2034 respectively.

HMS Defender

DESTROYERS
DARING CLASS (Type 45)

Ship	Pennant Number	Completion Date	Builder
DARING	D32	2008	BVT Surface Fleet
DAUNTLESS	D33	2008	BVT Surface Fleet
DIAMOND	D34	2009	BVT Surface Fleet
DRAGON	D35	2011	BVT Surface Fleet
DEFENDER	D36	2012	BVT Surface Fleet
DUNCAN	D37	2013	BVT Surface Fleet

Displacement: 7,350 tonnes Dimensions: 152.4m x 21.2m x 5.7m Machinery: Integrated Electric Propulsion; 2 RR WR-21 GT alternators, 67,600 hp (49.7 MW); 2 Wärtsilä DG (4 MW); 2 Converteam motors (40 MW); 2 shafts Speed: 29 knots Armament: 1 - 4.5-inch gun, 2 x Quad Harpoon missile launchers (on four ships), Sea Viper missile system comprising Sylver VLS with combination of up to 48 Aster 15 and Aster 30 missiles, 2 x Vulcan Phalanx (fitted as required) Aircraft: Wildcat or Merlin Complement: 190 (with space for 235)

Notes: These six vessels were originally planned to replace the preceding Type 42 destroyers on a ship-for-ship basis, but the original plan to buy twelve (down from 14 Type 42s) was cut to 8 and then finally six in June 2008, with all these ships entering service by 2013.

Central to the success of the design is its 18,000mph Sea Viper anti-aircraft missile system which can knock out enemy targets at ranges up to 70 miles from the ship. This potent weapon is linked to the powerful Sampson Multi-Function Radar that can track hundreds of targets at previously unheard distances of over 200 miles in all directions. With these key systems the six-destroyers, it was claimed at the time of their inception, could cover more surface area than a comparable Type 42 and thus fewer hulls were required. Or could it have been the £1 billion price tag for each of the new warships?

The Type 45s are incredibly spacious for the 190 men and women who serve aboard them, and the destroyers can play a defining role in the outcome of a full spectrum of military activities from full-scale naval operations, drug interdiction, maritime security, high seas piracy and intelligence gathering to Disaster Relief missions worldwide.

The Type 45 destroyers have received an unhealthy amount of criticism over the perceived weakness of their propulsion plants over the last few years. As long ago as 2016 the Government admitted that the Northrop Grumman intercooler was unreliable and prone to breaking down, particularly in hot and dry conditions. The solution was settled upon with a March 2018 announcement stating that Cammell Laird shipyard in Birkenhead would undertake restorative refits on all six ships by replacing their faulty diesel engines with three new ones, therefore adding another layer of redundancy into the system. This series of initiatives was christened 'The Power Improvement Project for the Type 45'. That it has taken five years to find a workable solution is disappointing.

DARING continues to languish at Portsmouth, unfit to return to sea, while DAUNTLESS, the second of class, has been in "extended refit" in Portsmouth since her last deployment to the Arabian Gulf in 2015 and has been relegated to the role of training ship for the past four years.

At the beginning of 2021, DAUNTLESS re-entered service having completed what was christened 'Upkeep 2020'. During this process, the destroyer was dry-docked and her undersides were painted with a special self-cleaning paint that eliminates the growth of marine life; an estimated 200-plus underwater value motors and valves were refurbished or replaced as were the ship's two propellors and 4.5inch gun forward. The shipyard also carried out work on over 2,000 smaller jobs ranging in size from fixing taps and door handles, to the installation of two new radar sets, including the latest version of the S1850M long range radar which can track up to 1,000 air targets at around 400 kilometres in 3D.

In early 2021 DEFENDER undertook a specialist training programme to enable her to provide the 'ring of steel' around the Queen Elizabeth Carrier Strike Group on her deployment to the Far East in 2021. She, with sister ship DIAMOND, will form a strong layered defensive screen around the aircraft carrier. The impact of the COVID-19 Pandemic on Royal Navy training in preparation for this deployment was keenly felt and some interesting and innovative solutions were found. One was for the ships of the Carrier Strike Group to undertake training virtually during the digital Exercise Virtual Warrior whilst alongside at Portsmouth. The exercise saw DEFENDER's crew play out a simulated crisis at HMS COLLINGWOOD that tested the capabilities and abilities of DEFENDER's and ELIZABETH's ships' companies.

FRIGATES
TYPE 23 (ASW Variant)

Ship	Pennant Number	Completion Date	Builder
KENT	F78	2000	Yarrow
PORTLAND	F79	2000	Yarrow
SUTHERLAND	F81	1997	Yarrow
SOMERSET	F82	1996	Yarrow
ST ALBANS	F83	2001	Yarrow
WESTMINSTER	F237	1993	Swan Hunter
NORTHUMBERLAND	F238	1994	Swan Hunter
RICHMOND	F239	1994	Swan Hunter

Displacement: 4,900 tonnes **Dimensions:** 133m x 16.1m x 5.5m **Machinery:** CODLAG; 2 RR Spey GT, 31,100 hp (23.2 MW); 4 Paxman diesels 8,100 hp (6 MW); 2 GEC motors, 4,000 hp (3 MW); 2 shafts **Speed:** 28 knots **Armament:** Harpoon or Sea Ceptor; 1 x 4.5-inch gun, 2 x single 30mm guns, 2 x twin (324 mm) Sting Ray Torpedo Tubes **Aircraft:** Wildcat or Merlin helicopter **Complement:** 185

Notes: The Type 23 provide the backbone to the Royal Navy's surface fleet, and whilst primarily designed for the anti-submarine warfare conditions found at the end of the Cold War, they have proven to be capable general-purpose vessels in the new technologically dominated battlespace. When originally conceived in the early 1980s, the Type 23 was to have been a relatively limited, affordable escort, but following the lessons of the

Falklands War of 1982, the design was recast and grew out of all recognition to the first simple design concepts. With this extra growth came a parallel increase in the cost of acquisition of platforms, and while the original ships had an expected service life of little more than twelve years, that figure now encompasses the age of the oldest Type 23, ARGYLL to the newest, ST ALBANS.

The Royal Navy's ambition is to keep these relatively old vessels at the forefront of technology and to bridge the gap between the first of the class leaving service and the introduction into service of the first of the new Type 26 City-class frigates from around 2025. To achieve this, the ships have received a LIFEX (Life Extension) programme of retrofits. This capability sustainment includes, but is not limited to, the removal of the legacy Seawolf anti-aircraft missile and its replacement with the more modern and capable Seaceptor missiles, extensive hull maintenance, and weapon and sensor upgrades to allow the ships to keep pace with the latest military developments around the globe.

Crucial to the LIFEX programme is work on the ship's Power Generation Machinery Upgrade (PGMU) which involves the replacement of four main propulsion diesel generator sets. Another, less well publicised aspect of the refit, is the installation of new 'stealth' technologies designed to assist in the detection of enemy deep submerged submarines, and furthermore, means to defend the frigates from detection themselves by the very submarines they are tracking. Work on the Type 23s has all been carried out at Babcock's at Devonport Dockyard where over 1,000 people work on the programme for the Ministry of Defence with each ship programme usually taking between 18-24 months to complete.

LANCASTER and RICHMOND were returned to the fleet in 2019. In early 2021 PORTLAND returned to service for the first time in four years following an extensive refit undertaken at Devonport that saw her IT systems extensively overhauled. SOMERSET is still undergoing refit at Devonport and is expected to complete the last Type 23 LIFEX refit in 2021. KENT and RICHMOND have been given the honour of deploying to the Far East as part of the escort group for the QUEEN ELIZABETH Carrier Group deployment in 2021.

The planned decommissioning dates are: WESTMINSTER (2028); NORTHUMBERLAND (2029); RICHMOND (2030); SOMERSET (2031); SUTHERLAND (2032); KENT (2033); PORTLAND (2034) and ST ALBANS (2035).

HMS Lancaster

FRIGATES
TYPE 23 (GP Variant)

Ship	Pennant Number	Completion Date	Builder
LANCASTER	F229	1991	Yarrow
ARGYLL	F231	1991	Yarrow
IRON DUKE	F234	1992	Yarrow
MONMOUTH	F235	1993	Yarrow
MONTROSE	F236	1993	Yarrow

Displacement: 4,900 tonnes **Dimensions:** 133m x 16.1m x 5.5m **Machinery:** CODLAG; 2 RR Spey GT, 31,100 hp (23.2 MW); 4 Paxman diesels 8,100 hp (6 MW); 2 GEC motors, 4,000 hp (3 MW); 2 shafts **Speed:** 28 knots **Armament:** Harpoon or Sea Ceptor; 1 - 4.5-inch gun, 2 x single 30mm guns, 2 x twin (324 mm) Sting Ray Torpedo Tubes **Aircraft:** Wildcat or Merlin helicopter **Complement:** 185

Notes: These ships operate in the General-Purpose role within the Royal Navy structure and have not been retrofitted with the advanced Type 2037 sonar system. As these ships are the oldest Type 23s in the fleet it is expected that they will be the first to be replaced by the new Type 31 frigates when they enter service.

In 2019 IRON DUKE was towed to Plymouth for her LIFEX refit that is expected to see her fitted with a new 3D Artisan radar and air defence weapon system and Sea Ceptor missiles replacing her legacy Seawolf. MONMOUTH was scheduled to have entered refit in early 2019 but this was initially delayed with her crew becoming the starboard crew for the forward deployed MONTROSE. Both frigates are being withdrawn early following the publication of the Integrated Defence Review.

MONMOUTH will leave service by the end of 2021 and MONTROSE by early 2022. Originally they were expected to continue to serve until 2026 and 2027, respectively. This will reduce the Type 23 fleet to just 11 vessels. Three are undergoing refit at Devonport (SUTHERLAND, IRON DUKE AND ST ALBANS). Three have largely completed refits and either are, or will shortly be, undergoing sea trials (RICHMOND, PORTLAND and SOMERSET). The number of operational Type 23 frigates is now six with MONMOUTH out of action entirely.

The Type 23s will be replaced over the next ten years with eight Type 26 and five Type 31 frigates. Construction of the latter will commence at Rosyth later this year. The programme is due to complete by 2027. The out-of-service dates for the remaining three ships remain ARGYLL (2023), LANCASTER (2024) and IRON DUKE (2025).

Early 2021, MONTROSE was back on station in the Arabian Gulf after completing a Fleet Time Support Programme in Oman. The work took place at Duqm Naval Dockyard (DND), a specialised naval repair and maintenance facility located within the massive Oman Drydocks facility at Duqm, on the Arabian Sea.

MONTROSE's four-week alongside maintenance period saw essential repairs and performance improvements carried out to the frigate and involved more than 250 critical elements in the scope of work. By using DND to undertake this work, the RN got an on-time, on-budget turnaround of the frigate to return on operational deployment in the Arabian Gulf and Indian Ocean, without MONTROSE having to return to the UK for the work.

Early 2021, after over two years inside the 'Frigate Sheds' at the Frigate Support Centre in HMNB Devonport, Type 23 frigate SOMERSET emerged and was moved to 2 Basin.

● CROWN COPYRIGHT/MOD   **HMS Somerset**

HMS Montrose

FRIGATES
CITY CLASS (Type 26)

Ship	Pennant Number	Completion Date	Builder
GLASGOW	-	-	BAE Systems Glasgow
CARDIFF	-	-	BAE Systems Glasgow
BELFAST	-	-	BAE Systems Glasgow
Batch 2			
BIRMINGHAM	-	-	BAE Systems Glasgow
SHEFFIELD	-	-	BAE Systems Glasgow
NEWCASTLE	-	-	BAE Systems Glasgow
LONDON	-	-	BAE Systems Glasgow
EDINBURGH	-	-	BAE Systems Glasgow

Displacement: 8,000+ tonnes full load Dimensions: 149.9m x 20.8m Machinery: CODLOG; 2 shafts Speed: 26 knots Range: 7,000 nautical miles Armament: 12-cell VLS for 48 Sea Ceptor anti-air missiles, 24-cell Mk 41 VLS for Tomahawk, 1 x 5inch 62 calibre Mk 45 naval gun, 2 x 30mm DS30M Mk2 guns, 2 x Phalanx CIES, 2 x miniguns, 4 x general purpose machine guns Aircraft: up to two helicopters (Wildcat) armed with 4 x anti-ship missiles, or 2 anti-submarine torpedoes, 20 Martlet multi-role air-to-surface missiles and Mk 11 depth charges or 1 x Merlin armed with 4 anti-submarine torpedoes Complement: 157 (with space for 208)

Notes: The long drawn-out timeframe associated with the design and development of modern warships is plain to see in the development of the Type 26 or City Class frigates. Planning for the replacement of the Type 22 and Type 23 frigates of the surface fleet started in 1998 with the commencement of the Future Surface Combatant (FSC) programme. The research trimaran RV TRITON was procured, but in the end more conventional hull designs were chosen over radical innovations. In March 2005, two versions of the FSC were announced showing a two-class series of ships, one 'Medium Sized Vessel Derivative' for service in the 2016-19 timeframe, and a more capable 'Versatile Surface Combatant' entering service from around 2023.

Circa 2006 defence officials, trying to get the best bang for their buck, explored the possibilities of extracting the maximum synergies between the FSC and the need for replacement survey ships and minesweepers under the Sustained Surface Combatant Capability (S2C2) programme. There were three clear requirements for the Royal Navy at this time: C1 - a high-end anti-submarine dedicated vessel of around 6,000 tonnes displacement; C2 - a general purpose platform of around 4-5,000 tonnes and C3 - a Global Corvette which could replace most of the survey and minewarfare fleet in service.

In 2008 the FSC concept was brought forward in the budget at the expense of building another pair of Type 45 destroyers. Detailed design work on the new C1 and C2 concepts was handed over to BAE Systems in 2009. Each vessel would have an expected lifespan of 25 years with one being built every year for a total of 18 (10C1 and 8C2 variants).

Crucially, the first of the FSCs were to have entered service in 2020. In 2020 the minewarfare aspect of the programme was dropped in favour of the Mine Countermeasures, Hydrography and Patrol Capability (MHPC) programme. In 2010 FSC became the Global Combat Ship and expectations were high that the first of class might be in service by 2021. 2010, however, was the year when the Strategic Defence and Security Review stripped the Royal Navy of the highly capable Type 22 frigates, the ARK ROYAL, and the Harrier jump jets. Orders for new ships were farmed off into the long grass for a while and the programme started to slip. The Government's decision to reduce the size of the surface fleet to just 19 escorts also meant there would be fewer orders for the Global Combat Ship. The Government also insisted that the specifications for the Global Combat Ship be pared down on a cost saving exercise from around £500m per ship to closer to £250m - £350m. However, this decision was later recinded and in February 2015 BAE Systems signed a £859m MOD contract to continue development and work towards manufacture. Ultimately, on 2 July 2017 BAE Systems was awarded a £3.7 billion contract to build the first three ships at their Govan shipyard on the Clyde.

In design, the Global Combat Ship has modularity and flexibility as key capability enhancers to allow the ships to operate in as wider range of scenarios as possible, from full-scale war to maritime security, counter piracy and humanitarian relief. Through-life support offered by BAE Systems is another key component in ensuring that the hulls remain relevant throughout the next three decades, as technology develops, and can be replaced relatively easily. The Royal Navy Type 26 ships will be equipped with the Type 997 Artisan 3D search radar and the Sea Ceptor (CAMM) anti-air-defence missile system launched via 48 vertical launch system (VLS) canisters. An additional 24-cell Mk 41 'strike length VLS' cells are positioned forward of the bridge and can accommodate long-range strike weapons such as Tomahawk land-attack cruise missiles and future long-range supersonic anti-ship and anti-land weapons. The City class's primary role remains that of anti-submarine warfare and for this the ships' hulls have been designed to be acoustically quiet. They are equipped with powerful Ultra Electronics Type 2150 next generation bow mounted sonar and a Sonar 2087 towed array. Each ship will be up-gunned from the current 4.5inch calibre gun of the Type 23s and Type 45s to mount a NATO standard BAE 5inch, 62 calibre Mk 45 naval gun. For propulsion, the Type 26s will feature a gas turbine direct drive and four high speed diesel generators driving a pair of electric motors in a combined diesel-electric or gas (CODLOG) configuration.

The first of class was named GLASGOW, with steel being cut in her construction on 20 July 2017.

The Type 26 design has been chosen by Canada and Australia as the basis for their frigate replacement programmes, respectively the Canadian Surface Combatant and the Hunter Class. Canada is building up to 15 ships and Australia nine. Both nations are procuring many more hulls than the Royal Navy.

BAE SYSTEMS

• BAE SYSTEMS

Future HMS Glasgow

HMS Chiddingfold

MINE COUNTERMEASURES SHIPS (MCMV)
HUNT CLASS

Ship	Pennant Number	Completion Date	Builder
LEDBURY	M30	1981	Vosper T
CATTISTOCK	M31	1982	Vosper T
BROCKLESBY	M33	1983	Vosper T
MIDDLETON	M34	1984	Yarrow
CHIDDINGFOLD	M37	1984	Vosper T
HURWORTH	M39	1985	Vosper T

Displacement: 750 tonnes FL **Dimensions:** 60m x 10.5m x 3.4m **Machinery:** 2 Caterpillar C32 ACERT diesels; 1 Deltic 9-55B diesel for pulse generator and auxiliary drive; 2 shafts; 1 bow thruster **Speed:** 15 knots **Armament:** 1 x 30mm; 2 x Miniguns **Complement:** 45 crew and 5 officers

Notes: With the introduction of new autonomous methods of dealing with the threat posed by sea mines, the future for the mine countermeasures vessels of the Hunt Class would seem, on paper, to be limited. Under current plans, over the next few years the oldest members of the class will be retired from service and replaced with autonomous systems that can be remotely operated from a wide variety of naval vessels from a safe distance removing the danger to life posed by these weapons. The oldest member of the fleet LEDBURY, entered service as long ago as 1980, but regular retrofits have enabled the ship to remain current when faced with an increasingly technologically advanced threat that is becoming more deadly and harder to combat with each successive year.

Two members of the class, CHIDDINGFOLD and BROCKLESBY, are forward deployed to the Persian Gulf to provide a permanent Royal Navy presence together with two Sandown-class minehunters as part of Operation Kipion. The four MCMVs use highly trained Mine Clearance Divers and the SeaFox unmanned mine disposal system to detect and neutralise mines.

In April 2020 MIDDLETON returned to the water in Portsmouth Naval Base after spending six months being refitted in BAE Systems large Shipbuilding Hall. The GRP-hulled MCMV is now about to enter her 37th year of service with the RN after being returned to the water via the semi-submersible barge Skylift 3000. The £7.5 million refit saw HMS Middleton being fitted with improved diesel generators, along with upgraded hull and crew accommodation. The BAE Systems team completed over 65,000 production hours on the MCMV including a full structural re-baselining of the ship with over two miles of laminating cloth being laid, extensive system enhancements undertaken, as well as maintenance and defect rectification.

The Hunt Class will be replaced in service by new autonomous minewarfare vessels that are cheaper and more expendable than manned vessels. The Royal Navy is working with their French counterparts in the development of a £117 million Maritime Mine Counter Measures (MMCM). It is expected that the last of the Hunt Class will leave service by 2025.

CROWN COPYRIGHT/MOD

HMS Ledbury

HMS Grimsby

SANDOWN CLASS

Ship	Pennant Number	Completion Date	Builder
PENZANCE	M106	1998	Vosper T
PEMBROKE	M107	1998	Vosper T
GRIMSBY	M108	1999	Vosper T
BANGOR	M109	2000	Vosper T
RAMSEY	M110	2000	Vosper T
BLYTH	M111	2001	Vosper T
SHOREHAM	M112	2001	Vosper T

Displacement: 600 tonnes Dimensions: 52.5m x 10.9m x 2.3m Machinery: 2 Paxman Valenta diesels, 1,523 hp; Voith-Schneider propulsion; 2 bow thrusters Speed: 13 knots Armament: 1 x 30mm gun; 2 x Miniguns; 3 x GPMG Complement: 34

Notes: The Sandown-class Mine Counter Measure Vessels are based in Scotland. The staff and ships of Mine Counter Measures 1 (MCM1) Squadron deploy in the Northern Gulf, conduct NATO exercises with other nations and work around the British Coastline, protecting the United Kingdom's shores and clearing the old ordnance that remains as a legacy of previous wars.

PENZANCE and SHOREHAM are forward deployed to the Persian Gulf in support of Operation Kipion. There they operate with two Hunt-class vessels CHIDDINGFOLD and

BROCKLESBY and their support ship RFA CARDIGAN BAY. This RN group's role is to ensure the safe passage of cargoes through the vital Hormuz Straits in the Persian Gulf and deter the laying of offensive mines to block the free transfer of goods and services.

The seven Sandown-class vessels are to be gradually replaced in service by new unmanned autonomous mine disposal systems by the end of the 2020s. The Sandown Class will be retired before the more capable Hunt-class vessels. These ships are still comparatively young, and it is very likely that they will be sold abroad for further service.

CROWN COPYRIGHT/MOD   **HMS Shoreham**

CROWN COPYRIGHT/MOD   **HMS Bangor**

CROWN COPYRIGHT/MOD

MARITIME MINE
COUNTERMEASURES SYSTEMS (MMCS)

Displacement: 6,000 kg Dimensions: 11m x 3.2m x 0.5m Payload: 4 tonnes Speed: 40+ knots
Complement: cabin for crew but usually unmanned

Notes: On 20 January 2021, the MOD awarded Atlas Elektronik UK a £25 million contract to deliver Great Britain's first unmanned minesweeper. Two further vessels will be delivered against the contract that will utilise autonomous, more expendable vessels against the deadly threat posed by sea mines.

RNMB HEBE, named after the ancient Greek goddess of youth, has joined sister vessels HARRIER and HAZARD as part of the Royal Navy's crewless mine-hunting programme Project Wilton. Hebe (in the background) is four metres longer than her sisters and with more technology on board (hence the extended cabin).

The new vessels use a system of cutting-edge technologies known as a 'Combined Influence Sweep' which has been developed to combat modern digital sea mines that are more sophisticated than their pressure, acoustic and contact system predecessors. The uncrewed boats will tow innovative Coiled Auxiliary Boats (CABs) which are made from a novel 'Drop Stitch' inflatable panel material. Onboard the CABs are systems which can generate a variety of simulated signal influences to initiate the mine harmlessly away from ships. The system is controlled remotely at a safe distance on a nearby ship or even many miles away on land.

The first (Sweep) system will be delivered in 2022 and will gradually replace conventional minehunters in the fleet, starting with the Sandown Class.

HMS Trent

PATROL VESSELS
RIVER II CLASS

Ship	Pennant Number	Completion Date	Builder
FORTH	P222	2018	BAE Systems
MEDWAY	P223	2019	BAE Systems
TRENT	P224	2019	BAE Systems
TAMAR	P233	2019	BAE Systems
SPEY	P234	2019	BAE Systems

Displacement: 2,000 tonnes **Dimensions:** 90.5m x 13.5m x 3.8m **Speed:** 24 knots **Armament:** 1 x 30mm cannon; 2 x Miniguns, 2 x GPMG **Aviation:** Flight deck capable of receiving aircraft up to Merlin size **Complement:** 36 (accommodation for 70)

Notes: The River II Class were developed from the previous River Class but are significantly more advanced and larger with far greater capabilities including the addition of a flight deck capable of accommodating a Merlin helicopter; a capability that has been tested on MEDWAY during her current Caribbean deployment. Each of the River IIs feature enhanced firefighting equipment, BAEs CMS-1 combat management system, an I Band Doppler SharpEye radar for helicopter control, and improved accommodation. In fact, the bridge of a River II-class patrol vessel compares extremely favourably against a Type 45 destroyer or Type 23 frigate with plenty of space for personnel.

Prime Minister Boris Johnson's ambition of making the Royal Navy the most capable and influential European Navy relies on the abilities of these vessels to a very large extent.

His government wants to have the Royal Navy in as many places as possible for as long as possible extending a presence beyond Britain's shores. Already, MEDWAY deployed in January 2020 to the Caribbean offering hurricane support, drug interdiction and COVID-19 pandemic relief efforts across the region. In September 2020 MEDWAY together with RFA ARGUS and the US Coast Guard intercepted drug smugglers trying to land cocaine with a street value of £81 million.

FORTH is permanently deployed to the Falkland Islands having replaced the previous Falkland Islands Guardship CLYDE at the end of 2019. On 31 March 2021, TRENT sailed from Portsmouth to Gibraltar where she became the Royal Navy's first forward deployed patrol vessel in the Mediterranean. The last of the five River II class, SPEY was commissioned into the Royal Navy on 7 January 2021. She and sister ship TAMAR are likely to also be deployed around the globe with one possibly positioned in the Far East, most likely at Singapore.

It has been suggested that the armament of the Forth Class would be greatly improved with a 57mm gun mounted forward, two 30mm cannons and a five-cell missile pannier fitted to all three guns capable of launching the Martlett missile. This is an 8km-range variant of the Thales lightweight multi-role missile. These improvements would transform a lightly-armed OPV into a formidable gunboat or corvette.

During a maintenance period at A&P shipyard in Falmouth, engineers added a 'dazzle camouflage' paint job to TAMAR's hull for the first time since the Second World War.

GORDON BRODIE

HMS Tamar

HMS Mersey

PATROL VESSELS
RIVER CLASS

Ship	Pennant Number	Completion Date	Builder
TYNE	P281	2002	Vosper T
SEVERN	P282	2003	Vosper T
MERSEY	P283	2003	Vosper T

Displacement: 1,677 tonnes Dimensions: 79.5m x 13.6m x 3.8m Machinery: 2 MAN 12RK 270 diesels, 11,063 hp; 2 shafts; bow thruster Speed: 20+ knots Armament: 1 x 20mm; 2 x GPMG Complement: 48

Notes: These three ships were originally ordered from Vosper Thornycroft in 2001 on a then unusual deal whereby the Royal Navy leased them from the shipbuilder for five years at a cost of £60 million. A £52 million lease extension was agreed in January 2007 running to the end of 2013. The Ministry of Defence in 2012 authorised the purchase of the three ships from the shipbuilder for the price of £39 million. The MOD intended to keep them operational for another ten years through to 2022.

For a while it was expected that the new River II Class would replace them in service. SEVERN was decommissioned in October 2017 but with the current Government's foreign policy statement on having dispersed naval assets around the globe the River IIs have been forward deployed leaving their older, smaller, and less capable sister ships to maintain the round the clock protection of Great Britain's borders and vital Fishery Protection Role.

In November 2018, the then Defence Secretary Gavin Williamson, announced that the future of these three ships was secure for a few extra years, but their future, or any replacements, other than the five RIVER IIs are unclear at the present time.

SEVERN joins her sisters MERSEY and TYNE with the capabilities and training to escort passing foreign warships, mount fishing vessel inspections and defend the UK border. She also performs a unique role providing training for Royal Navy navigators who join the ship for testing pilotage off the west coast of Scotland and English Channel.

● CROWN COPYRIGHT/MOD

HMS Tyne

● DAVE CULLEN

COASTAL TRAINING CRAFT
P2000 CLASS

Ship	Pennant Number	Completion Date	Builder
EXPRESS	P163	1988	Vosper T
EXPLORER	P164	1985	Watercraft
EXAMPLE	P165	1985	Watercraft
EXPLOIT	P167	1988	Vosper T
ARCHER	P264	1985	Watercraft
BITER	P270	1985	Watercraft
SMITER	P272	1986	Watercraft
PURSUER	P273	1988	Vosper T
TRACKER	P274	1998	Ailsa Troon
RAIDER	P275	1998	Ailsa Troon
BLAZER	P279	1988	Vosper T
DASHER	P280	1988	Vosper T

Ship	Pennant Number	Completion Date	Builder
PUNCHER	P291	1988	Vosper T
CHARGER	P292	1988	Vosper T
RANGER	P293	1988	Vosper T
TRUMPETER	P294	1988	Vosper T

Displacement: 54 tonnes Dimensions: 20.8m x 5.8m x 1.8m Machinery: 2 Caterpillar C18 diesels, 1,746 hp; 2 MTU diesels, 2,000 hp (TRACKER); 2 shafts Speed: 20 knots Armament: 3 x GPMG (Faslane based vessels) Complement: 5 (with accommodation for up to 12).

Notes: These fourteen vessels are among the oldest Royal Navy units dating from the mid-1980s, but there are currently no plans for their replacement. Their role is to train future command personnel and most of the class are attached to University Royal Naval Units (URNU), but can also contribute to numerous other naval tasks around the waters of the United Kingdom and into European waters. Commodore Britannia Royal Naval College has overall responsibility for the URNUs whose role is to educate and inform a wide spectrum of high calibre undergraduates.Vessels are assigned to the following URNUs, ARCHER (East Scotland); BITER (Manchester & Salford), BLAZER (Southampton); CHARGER (Liverpool); EXAMPLE (Northumbria); EXPLOIT (Birmingham); EXPLORER (Yorkshire); EXPRESS (Wales); PUNCHER (London); RANGER (Sussex); SMITER (Oxford); TRUMPETER (Cambridge).

Two vessels – PURSUER and DASHER - formed the Cyprus Squadron from 2003 to 2010. Both returned to the UK in April 2010 to form the Faslane Patrol Boat Squadron, performing security duties within HMNB Clyde. In 2012 they were replaced by the last two P2000 vessels built - RAIDER and TRACKER. They are fully-fledged armed patrol boats and fitted with Kevlar armour and able to mount three 7.62mm General Purpose Machine Guns (GPMG). They are part of a growing Force Protection cadre based at Faslane to protect the UKs nuclear deterrent. These two vessels are fully engaged in FP duties and do not undertake university training.

RANGER and TRUMPETER were formerly allocated to the Gibraltar Squadron for guard ship and search and rescue duties, but were replaced by the dedicated Scimitar Class. Unlike the remainder of the class, both these ships remain capable of being mounted with a 20mm cannon.

In 2020 DASHER and PURSUER replaced SCIMITAR and SABRE as the Gibraltar Squadron. They in turn will be replaced by the new Gibraltar Fast Patrol Boats being built on Merseyside by Marine Specialist Technology.

HMS Sabre

SCIMITAR CLASS

Ship	Pennant Number	Completion Date	Builder
SCIMITAR	P284	1988	Halmatic
SABRE	P285	1988	Halmatic

Displacemen:t 24 tonnes Dimensions: 16m x 4.7m x 1.4m Machinery: 2 MAN V10 diesels, 740 hp; 2 shafts Speed: 27+ knots Armament: 2 x GPMG Complement: 5 ratings and 1 officer

Notes: These two vessels were originally built by Halmatic (now part of BAE Systems) as Lifespan Patrol Vessels (LPVs) for secret services in Northern Ireland. They were given the names MV GREY FOX and MV GREY WOLF. In this capacity they were capable of a top speed of 30 knots and armed with two General Purpose Machine Guns (GPMGs). Acquired by the Royal Navy in 2003, they were shipped to Gibraltar to bolster the colony's defences and provide fast vessels that could interdict smugglers and escort high value ships and warships through the Straits of Gibraltar.

In June 2020, the two ships were transported back to the United Kingdom where they have supplemented the training role performed by the ARCHER P2000 boats with University URNUs.

At 24 tonnes displacement they continue to hold the title of the smallest commissioned Royal Navy vessels currently in service.

Fast Patrol Boats

GIBRALTAR SQUADRON
FAST PATROL BOATS

Ship	Pennant Number	Completion Date	Builder
DAGGER	-	2021	Marine Specialised Tech
CUTLASS	-	2022	Marine Specialised Tech

Dimensions: 19m in length   **Machinery:** 3 x Volvo D13-1000 engines driving 3 x MJP350X waterjets **Speed:** up to 40+ knots   **Armament:** 3 x General Purpose Machine Guns (fitted for but not with 0.50cal Heavy Machine Gun)   **Complement:** 6

Notes: These two vessels are the replacements for SCIMITAR and SABRE. In July 2020, the Ministry of Defence contracted Merseyside based boat builder Marine Specialised Technology (MTS) to build a pair of new boats for the Gibraltar Squadron in a deal worth £9 million. Both boats will be used to patrol HMNB Gibraltar and British Gibraltar Territorial Waters (BGTW) as well as supporting British exercises and operations in the area, keeping a close watch over Gibraltar's shores.

The first vessel will enter service in the third quarter of 2021 and the second expected to join her in the first quarter of 2022.

The Gibraltar Squadron also operates a trio of Rigid Hull Inflatable Boats (RHIBs) and the recently allocated River II-class patrol ship TRENT.

● DEREK FOX   **HMS Scott**

SURVEY SHIPS
SCOTT CLASS

Ship	Pennant Number	Completion Date	Builder
SCOTT	H131	1997	Appledore

Displacement: 13,500 tonnes   Dimensions: 131.5m x 21.5m x 8.3m   Machinery: 2 Krupp MaK 9M32 diesels, 10,800 hp; 1 shaft, CP propeller; retractable bow thruster   Speed: 17 knots   Complement: 78

Notes: SCOTT is nearing the end of her Royal Navy career having first commissioned in 1997. She was built to commercial standards and continues to provide extremely accurate and detailed deep bathymetric surveys of the continental shelf. She is fitted with modern multi-beam sonar suite with which she can conduct ocean mapping operations on a global scale.

Onboard, her 78 crew members operate a three-watch system whereby the ship is run by 48 of her crew with the remainder on leave at any given time. Each person aboard works 75 days on the ship before having 30 days ashore. In this way SCOTT can remain at sea for more than 300 days a year consolidating the work she has undertaken and avoiding unnecessary wasteful breaks in the surveying. She can navigate through thin Ice Class 1A conditions, but only with the assistance of a dedicated icebreaker.

SCOTT is the largest survey vessel in Western Europe, and the fifth largest vessel in the Royal Navy. Named for the famous Arctic explorer Robert Falcon Scott, she also has an auxiliary role as a mine countermeasures vessel. After 24 to 25 years in service, out of service date for SCOTT has been set as 2022.

HMS Enterprise

ECHO CLASS

Ship	Pennant Number	Completion Date	Builder
ECHO	H87	2002	Appledore
ENTERPRISE	H88	2003	Appledore

Displacement: 3,500 tonnes **Dimensions:** 90.6m x 16.8m x 5.5.m **Machinery:** Diesel electric; 3 DG (4.8MW); 2 x azimuth thrusters, 2,279 hp (1.7 MW); 1 bow thruster **Speed:** 15 knots **Armament:** 2 x 20mm **Complement:** 48 (with accommodation for 81)

Notes: ECHO and ENTERPRISE are multi-role survey vessel – hydrographic oceanographic (SVHO)s. The two ships were built in Devon at Appledore Shipbuilders who had been subcontracted by prime contractors Vosper Thornycroft to build the ships. Their role is primarily one of survey and oceanographic research although they retain a secondary role as mine countermeasures HQ ships. Similar to other Royal Navy survey ships, these vessels spend most of their time at sea with the ship's company adopting a different working pattern to maintain them at sea. Of the crew of 72 on each ship, only about 48 are ever aboard, with the remainder on leave, training, or other duties.

The versatility of these vessels was proven in August 2020 when ENTERPRISE was dispatched from Cyprus to Beirut following a disastrous 2,750 tonnes nitrate explosion that levelled huge parts of the city killing more than 200 people, injuring thousands and leaving 300,000 homeless. She was part of a £5 million package of UK Government aid to the devastated city. Onboard the survey ship were mobile surveying kits that were used to assess the damage to the port infrastructure in the explosion.

More recently, she has surveyed hundreds of thousands of square miles of ocean floor and stood in as a temporary replacement for the Falkland Island's Patrol Vessel and acted as the flagship to the Standing NATO Mine Counter-Measures Group 2.

In recent months, ECHO spent time operating in the Baltic with the Lithuanian Navy and during her research discovered the wreck of the British cruiser CASSANDRA sunk in the Baltic by a mine. CASSANDRA was part of a force sent as part of the Allied intervention in the Russian Civil War to support the newly founded Baltic states of Latvia and Estonia against the Bolsheviks in 1918. CASSANDRA struck a mine on December 5, 1918 near the island of Saaremaa taking 400 of her crew down with her. Close by were the wrecks of two other Royal Navy ships MYRTLE and GENTIAN sunk on July 15, 1919.

CROWN COPYRIGHT/MOD

HMS Echo

HMS Protector

ICE PATROL SHIP
PROTECTOR

Ship	Pennant Number	Completion Date	Builder
PROTECTOR	A173	2001	Havyard Leirvik (Norway)

Displacement: 4,985 tonnes **Dimensions:** 89.7m x 18m x 7.25m **Machinery:** 2 Rolls Royce Bergen diesels, 9,602 hp; 1 shaft; CP propeller; bow and stern thrusters **Speed:** 15 knots **Armament:** Miniguns; GPMGs **Complement:** 88 (accommodation for up to 100)

Notes: In January 2021 PROTECTOR, the Royal Navy's only Ice Patrol Ship, re-emerged from a ten-month £14 million refit to enhance her capabilities. Usually found operating in the freezing waters of Antarctica and the Southern Hemisphere, PROTECTOR's ship's company includes a team of permanent divers who undertake exploratory surveys.

The latest refit is the longest and biggest in the ship's ten-year naval career having been undertaken at UK Docks on Teeside since March 2020. She spent five-months in dry dock having her hull inspected and repainted whilst her facilities aboard were enhanced. During the refit extra work previously unidentified in the initial surveys was discovered, meaning the ship required longer in dockyard hands than originally planned. The work package carried out on PROTECTOR included removal of the propellor shaft for inspection at a specialist company in Denmark and re-installation in the vessel, overhaul of all main and auxiliary diesel engines, and rebuilding of the quarterdeck to make more space available onboard.

The refit has been described as 'the most complex, demanding and transformative project'. PROTECTOR saw work carried out on her engines, generators, the creation of a new quarterdeck structure with a naval stores complex, new workshops to maintain the ship's two small survey craft JAMES CAIRD IV and the 8.5m Rigid Work Boat TERRA NOVA. She can also deploy two Pacific 22 RIBs (NIMROD and AURORA). She deploys with three BV206 all-terrain vehicles and four quad bikes and trailers to assist in moving stores and equipment.

The refit of PROTECTOR has resulted in more space being made available onboard the vessel for containers and supplies, which will be needed on the vessel's next deployment to Antarctica, which will see her take vital building supplies and fuel to help in the modernisation of the British Antarctic Survey science and research station at Rothera Point on Adelaide Island.

PROTECTOR will deploy to the Southern Ocean in late 2021 and will resume survey and scientific research missions across the region.

• CROWN COPYRIGHT/MOD

Survey Motor Boat JAMES CAIRD IV

HMS Magpie

INSHORE SURVEY VESSEL

Ship	Pennant Number	Completion Date	Builder
MAGPIE	H130	2018	Safehaven

Displacement: 37 tonnes **Dimensions:** 18m x 6.2m x 1.4m **Machinery:** 2 Volvo D16 diesels, 524 hp; 2 shafts **Speed:** 23 knots **Complement:** 12

Notes: MAGPIE replaced GLEANER in 2018 and has since then been actively surveying the inshore waters around the United Kingdom. She was purchased as one of 38 new workboats supplied by Atlas Elektronik and is unique in having a catamaran hull. She can operate offshore for up to 7 days with a crew of 12 and has a range of 1,400 nautical miles. Powered by twin Volvo D16 engines, the vessel has a 23kts maximum speed and survey speeds of 8-9kts.

In March 2020 MAGPIE was fitted with cutting edge software and electronics to keep her at the forefront of surveying technology allowing the survey ship to map the seabed close to shore not in days but in hours. The survey was in a position off Plymouth and was not as detailed as the scans usually taken by MAGPIEs hi-tech sonar suites, but the method developed by scientists from the National Oceanography Centre in Liverpool and MOD experts from Defence Science and Technology Laboratory could be extremely useful when time is of the essence, such as during times of war when surveys of the approaches to an enemy held anchorage or harbour are required with great speed.

Madfox

NAVYX MADFOX
UNMANNED SURFACE VESSEL

MADFOX, which stands for Maritime Demonstrator For Operational eXperimentation, was accepted into the Royal Navy in 2021 after being evaluated by the Defence Science and Technology Laboratory (Dstl) over a period of eighteen months. Based on the L3Harris Mast-13 autonomous vessel, MADFOX will be further evaluated by the Royal Navy in a variety of real-life scenarios to examine how autonomous vessels can deliver force multipliers, force protection and surveillance and reconnaissance assets to the fleet. For this next phase in its assessment process, the vessel will be under the control of the NavyX organisation that is tasked with evaluating new and innovative pieces of equipment for the Royal Navy.

NAVYX is also currently evaluating an autonomous Rigid Inflatable Boat (RIB) that will be incorporated into the inventory of the future Type 26 and Type 31 frigates.

Madfox

Royal Marine Craft

What is the future for the Royal Marines? In the last few months, the force has seen a radical transformation, not only in its organisation, its role, but even its uniform. The Future Commando Force (FCF) is the most comprehensive overhaul of the RM Commandos since the Second World War. However, details were released by the Government in 2021s Defence Command Paper including a £40 million injection into the Navy to develop the new FCF and British amphibious forces overall. Another £50 million will be used to convert a Bay-class landing support ship into a ship capable of delivering 'a more agile and lethal littoral strike capability'. But, some things will remain unchanged, including the spiritual home of the Commandos will still be at Plymouth even if the FCFs focus will increasingly become one of technical specialist operations.

The Future Commando Force will be swift, agile and nimble and be able to deploy rapidly around the globe at a moment's notice. They will be equipped with unique 'game changing technology, weaponry and equipment' unlike that used in any other units in the British armed forces and be capable of undertaking roles ranging from humanitarian aid, combat missions to full-scale warfighting. They will regularly deploy on attachment to the UK's Carrier Strike Groups, but also be retained in home waters. In July 2020, the Royal Marines created The Vanguard Strike Company, a new unit of more than 150 Marines and British Army Commandos.

To achieve the aim of increased agility company personnel will work in 'small, versatile teams' specially tailored for each individual mission. Each Marine will be specially selected by his individual skill sets allowing more autonomy of movement and decision at the company level. This could be as small as teams of four, as was tested by 40 Commando in 2020 at Bovington Training Area in Dorset. Larger groups have not been abandoned either with groups of 12 being trialled in October 2020 in Littoral Response Group (Experimentation) exercise held in Cyprus. During these exercises, the Royal Marines trialled drones to assist in mission planning, resupply, reconnaissance, and execution of the mission.

The Government's focus on forward deploying British forces abroad also applies to the Future Commando Force with the aim of establishing high readiness groups in warships and auxiliaries already on deployment. Major General Matt Holmes, Commandant General Royal Marines, said the new Vanguard Strike Company will "lead and inform" as the Royal Marines continue to "fight in a dynamic, technological era of warfare".

The Vanguard Strike Company will be deployed for the first time in mid-2021, and the company will be the first RM unit to wear the new Royal Marines Uniform procured from US firm Crye Precision. The new outfit was selected for the extreme environments RM personnel work in and includes new disruptive material shirts, trousers and water-proof jacket replacing the Gortex jacked currently used. The new uniform is lighter, stronger, faster-drying and more breathable than the existing uniform and has a slightly different camouflage pattern. Perhaps more symbolic than practical are the finer touches to the uniform. It will be the first time in decades that the Royal Marines are not sharing the same uniform as soldiers in the British Army and the familiar arched black and green RM shoulder flash will be replaced to a navy blue and red Velcro rectangular patch whose design dates from the Second World War.

Finally, if anyone was in any doubt where the Royal Marines loyalty lies, the Union Flag on the left arm is replaced by a White Ensign.

The Royal Marines will continue to operate landing craft from the assault ships BULWARK and ALBION and the Bay-class landing ships. Furthermore, they have a range of small fast inshore hovercraft and assault craft on which RM personnel are trained at Plymouth, Instow in North Devon and at HMS Raleigh at Torpoint. The latter location houses the Royal Navy School of Board and Search, which trains personnel in the special skills of boarding vessels underway that may restrict searches.

On 26 October 2020, SBS personnel were ordered to board a hijacked commercial ship, NAVE ANDROMEDA, in the Solent, when it had been taken over by hijackers. Seven people were detained within ten minutes of the British special forces landing on the deck, having been delivered by helicopter.

Future Commando Force will, it is hoped, add to the Royal Marines 'distinctive and unique capabilities' and reaffirm the Government's commitment to amphibious strike from the sea.

CROWN COPYRIGHT/MOD

ISLAND CLASS PATROL VESSELS

Ship	Pennant Number	Launch Date	Builder
RONA	-	2009	Holyhead Marine
MULL	-	2010	Holyhead Marine
EORSA	-	2014	Holyhead Marine

Displacement: 19.9 tonnes   **Dimensions:** 14.9m x 4.6m x 0.9m   **Machinery:** 2 Caterpillar diesels, 715 hp; 2 waterjets **Speed:** 33 knots **Armament:** 4 x GPMG **Complement:** 3

Notes: The Island-class patrol boats RONA and MULL were former Ministry of Defence Police vessels from the Clyde Marine Unit at HMNB Clyde, handed over to the Royal Marines in 2013. They were fitted with three new weapons mounts, extra protection and communications equipment and transferred to 43 Commando Fleet Protection Group Royal Marines for operation on the Clyde to escort high value units such as the Vanguard-class submarines. A third vessel, EORSA, was delivered direct from the builders.

Landing Craft Utility (LCU)

LCU Mk10

Ship	Pennant Number	Parent Unit	Builder
9730	1001	47 CRGRM	Ailsa, Troon
9731	1002	47 CRGRM	Ailsa, Troon
9732	1003	HMS ALBION	BAE Systems
9733	1004	HMS ALBION	BAE Systems
9734	1005	HMS ALBION	BAE Systems
9735	1006	HMS ALBION	BAE Systems
9736	1007	47 CRGRM	BAE Systems
9737	1008	47 CRGRM	BAE Systems
9738	1009	47 CRGRM	BAE Systems
9739	1010	47 CRGRM	BAE Systems

Displacement: 240 tonnes Dimensions: 29.82m x 7.7m x 1.70m Machinery: 2 MAN Diesels; 2 Schottel propulsors; 1 bow thruster Speed: 10 knots Armament: 2 x GPMG Complement: 7

Notes: LCU Mk10 (Landing Craft Utility) are operated by the Royal Marines and are a Ro-Ro style landing craft designed to operate from Albion-class LPDs or Landing Ship Dock Auxiliary (LSDA). Ordered in 1998 from Ailsa Troon, the fleet currently consists of ten vessels, with the first two delivered in 1999 and with the final vessels being accepted into service in 2003. The remainder were built by BAE Systems at Govan. Both ALBION and BULWARK are each capable of carrying four LCUs.

They have a 'drive-through' configuration, with ramps fore and aft and pilot house shifted to starboard. They are capable of transporting up to 120 fully equipped troops, one main battle tank or four large vehicles. With a range of around 600 nautical miles – more if auxiliary tanks are added – they are designed to operate independently for 14 days with a seven man Royal Marine crew in both arctic and tropical climates. All the crew members have bunk accommodation and there is a galley and store rooms.

CROWN COPYRIGHT/MOD

Mexeflote

Mexeflote

Dimensions: 38.66m x 12.4m x 1.54m **Speed:** 6.5 knots **Complement:** 6 Crew

Notes: The Mexeflote consists of multiple cells and engines that can be configured to provide a causeway, landing craft or Ramp Support Pontoon. It is capable of transferring vehicles and equipment up to 198 tonnes and is routinely deployed worldwide via LSDs of the Royal Fleet Auxiliary. The Mexeflote is the largest logistic landing craft in the military and is operated exclusively by the Royal Logistic Corps. The Mexeflote is highly versatile and has been deployed in support of the majority of operational deployments since the Falklands conflict.

Landing Craft Vehicle and Personnel (LCVP)

LCVP Mk5B

Ship	Pennant Number	Parent Unit	Builder
0202	B5	47 CRGRM	Babcock Marine
0203	NM	HMS ALBION	Babcock Marine
0204	B6	47 CRGRM	Babcock Marine
0205	P7	47 CRGRM	Babcock Marine
0338	T6	47 CRGRM	Babcock Marine
0339		HMS ALBION	Babcock Marine
0340	N2	HMS ALBION	Babcock Marine
0341	P9	47 CRGRM	Babcock Marine
0344		47 CRGRM	Babcock Marine
0345		47 CRGRM	Babcock Marine
0346	N3	HMS ALBION	Babcock Marine
0347		47 CRGRM	Babcock Marine
0353		47 CRGRM	Babcock Marine

Ship	Pennant Number	Parent Unit	Builder
0354		47 CRGRM	Babcock Marine
0355		47 CRGRM	Babcock Marine
0356	B8	47 CRGRM	Babcock Marine

Displacement: 24 tonnes Dimensions: 15.70m x 4.2m x 0.90m Machinery: 2 Volvo Penta diesels; 2 waterjets Speed: 25 knots Armament: 2 x GPMG Complement: 3

Notes: Designed to carry personnel and small vehicles, the first LCVP Mk5 (Landing Craft Vehicle and Personnel) was ordered in 1995 from Vosper Thornycroft and handed over in 1996. A further four were delivered in December 1996 with two more for training at RM Poole ordered in 1998. A further 16 were ordered from FBM Babcock Marine in 2001 with the final vessels being accepted into service in 2004. The Mk 5 can transport 8 tonnes of stores or a mix of 2 tonnes and 35 fully equipped troops, and operate from both ALBION and BULWARK. These vessels represent a significant improvement in capability over the preceding Mk4s with a greater range, lift and speed. They feature aluminium hulls and are powered by twin waterjets. Their design includes a rigid and enclosed windowed canopy and a ramp at the bow that lowers for rapid unloading. GPMGs can be mounted when needed. The primary role is the landing of vehicles, personnel and equipment onto potentially hostile shores. The secondary role is a general purpose support craft both between ships and ship to shore. The craft are capable of performing normal duties in conditions up to sea state 4 and run for cover up to sea state 5. Pennant numbers and parent units can change as the vessels are rotated through maintenance cycles.

• GORDON BRODIE   Landing Craft Vehicle and Personnel (LCVP)

CROWN COPYRIGHT/MOD

Landing Craft Air Cushion (LCAC)

GRIFFON 2400TD LCAC

Ship	Pennant Number	Completion Date	Builder
C21	-	2010	Griffon
C22	-	2010	Griffon
C23	-	2010	Griffon
C24	-	2010	Griffon

G.R.T. 6.8 tonnes   Dimensions: 13.4m x 6.8m   Machinery: 1 Deutz diesel, 585 hp
Speed: 45 knots   Range: 300 nm   Armament: 1 x GPMG   Complement: 2 Crew; 16
fully-equipped marines.

Notes: Officially known as the Landing Craft Air Cushion (Light), the so-called 'floating
fortress' can carry 16 marines and race across water, ice and mud. Operated by 539
Raiding Squadron, the 2400TD offers greater payload, performance and obstacle clearance
than the earlier 2000 TD craft. Centre sections of the cabin roof can be removed in
order to embark two 1 tonnes NATO pallets. Similiar to the 2000TD, the 2400TD's design
allows the user to reduce the width of the craft with foldable side decks allowing it to
be transported on a standard low loader truck or in the hold of a C-130 Hercules aircraft.
They can also operate directly from the well-deck of RN amphibious ships. They are
equipped with a 7.62mm General Purpose Machine Gun, HF and VHF radios, radar, GPS,
ballistic protection and a variety of specialised equipment. They also produce next to
no wake at high speed, which makes them more stealthy than traditional landing craft
and with their powerful engines, much faster. All four entered service by the end of 2010.

Offshore Raiding Craftt

OFFSHORE RAIDING CRAFT

Weight: 3.6 tonnes   **Dimensions:** 9.1m x 2.9m x 0.66m   **Machinery:** Twin Steyr MO256K43 250 bhp @ 4200rpm   **Propulsion:** Rolls Royce FF270 Waterjets **Speed:** 36 knots   **Armament:** 1x HMG/GPMG forward, 2 x GPMG/HMG/GMG/Minigun aft **Complement:** 2 and 8 troops

Notes: The Royal Marines operate two versions of the Offshore Raiding Craft (ORC), the Troop Carrying Variant (TCV) and Fire Support Variant (FSV). The ORC is an air portable surface manoeuvre craft designed for the rapid deployment of 8 fully equipped troops and 2 crew from over the horizon (30 miles) ship-to-shore and vice versa. They provide rapid movement of troops in coastal, estuarine, riverine and inland waters. She has an aluminium hull with a low draught to allow for safe, rapid beach insertions. To provide ballistic protection for her 2 crew and passengers optional armour panels can be fitted.She can be transported as under-slung load by Chinook and Merlin helicopters or air-transported inside a C130 Hercules transport plane. Around 39 ORCs are in service with the Royal Marines. The ORC is manufactured by Holyhead Marine of Anglesey, North Wales.

RIGID RAIDING CRAFT

Notes: The Royal Marines operate a large number of smaller Rigid-hulled and Rigid-Inflatable Craft for various assault, patrol and security duties. There are 5.2, 6.5 and 8 metre long versions. Rigid Raiders feature GRP (glass reinforced plastic) hulls and early varants featured single or twin outboard motors. A small team of men can carry the boats, even with engines attached, due to their lightweight construction. They can also be air-dropped out to sea. The latest RRC, the Mk3, is powered by a 240 hp inboard diesel engine but the Royal Marines might start replacing these with ORCs. They can carry up to eight troops. Rigid Raiders are manufactured by RTK Marine (now part of BAE Systems).

SPECIALIST CRAFT

In addition to the familiar Rigid Raiding Craft and Rigid Inflatable Boats other specialist vessels are available including the Fast Interceptor Craft (FIC) with a top speed of 60 knots. Back in July 2007 it was revealed that the Special Boat Service (SBS) were to take delivery of the so-called 'stealth boat'. The vessel is manufactured by Portsmouth-based VT Halmatic, which is now part of BAE Systems, but not much has been revealed about the vessel. The vessel has been spotted numerous times in waters off Poole, home of the SBS, and according to the BAE Systems Maritime website they are currently in service with UK Special Forces.

To maintain a low radar cross-section, external fittings such as raydomes, aerial fits and apertures on the craft are kept to a minimum. This results in low radar and heat signatures enabling a stealth capability. The specification of the boats in service with the UK Special Forces remain a mystery as there are numerous options not only for the propulsion lines (such as twin or triple petrol outboards through to twin diesel stern drives, twin diesel jet drives or twin Arneson surface drives) but also for the system facilities. Options include multiple fuel tank arrangements, water separator/primary filter within the engine compartment, electric and manual bilge systems with automatic sensing and high bilge alarms, fire and/or smoke detection system with visual/audible display on console and/or cabin, variety of navigation and communication systems available to end user specification, including, but not limited to, fully integrated intercom systems, radar, satcom and multiple radio installation.

All craft are air transportable with special trailers available to suit different aircraft including A400M, C130 and C17.

Three models are available 30, 40 and 180.
Dimensions - Model 30: 10.75m x 2.59m x 0.7m
Dimensions - Model 40: 13.07m x 2.83m x 0.82m
Dimensions - Model 180: 18.1m x 3.8m x 0.9m

SWIMMER DELIVERY VEHICLES

Swimmer Delivery Vehicles (SDV) are miniature submarines operated by Britain's Special Forces to insert commandos and others into frontline situations or to undertake clandestine work. The Royal Navy owns three SDV Mk8 Mod 1 versions which are used by the Special Boat Service.

The Mk8 is the same vehicle used by the United States Navy SEAL teams, although the SEALs are upgrading their SDVs with the Shallow Water Combat Submersible (SWCS), designated as the Mk 11 SDV. In 2018 the UK government announced the intention to purchase three replacement SWCS for their existing fleet of SDVs.

On January 14, 2021, the US Department of Defense announced that a foreign military sale request from Teledyne Brown Engineering, the manufacturers of the SWCS for US$39,211,704 firm-fixed price modification to an existing contract had been awarded. The buyer nation was not disclosed due to the secretive nature of the technology involved but is widely believed to be to honour the British contract.

Ships for the Future Fleet

TYPE 31e FRIGATE (Inspiration Class)

Born out of the 2010 Strategic Defence and Security Review and emerging from the Global Combat Ship, these future vessels will complement the Type 32 frigate and the more capable Type 26 frigates. They are expected to enter service in the late 2020s.

Five ships each costing £250 million apiece are planned to be built at Rosyth in Scotland at a brand new £31.5 million state-of-the-art, 147-metre long, 30-metre high, construction hall that can accommodate two frigates under construction side by side simultaneously. Ship construction in the halls is expected to commence in 2021 after the contract was awarded to Babcock Team 31 in November 2019. The Type 31e programme is the first so called Pathfinder programmes to be delivered under the terms of the new National Shipbuilding Strategy that hopes to create a steady drumbeat of warship construction work for the nation's shipyards over the next ten, twenty and thirty years.

The Government hopes that by re-energising the UK's maritime capability by embracing new and innovative shipbuilding solutions and build practices the Type 31 will support technology transfer throughout the network of suppliers both nationally and internationally.

The Type 31e is based on Babcock's Arrowhead 140 design with a displacement of 6000+ tonnes length overall of 138.7m, a beam of 19.8m and a draught of 5m. The design boast a 32+MW electric propulsion system capable of propelling the frigates at speeds of over 28 knots.

The Type 31e is widely envisaged to be configured as a complimentary warship to existing Royal Navy designs in service or under construction, sitting roughly between the high-end capabilities of the Type 26 frigates and Type 45 destroyers and the River II class Offshore Patrol Vessels. For this role, the Type 31e's will be armed with a Bofors 57mm Mk 3 naval gun, 40mm guns and the Sea Ceptor anti-air missile system in vertical launch tubes. Each frigate will have a dedicated helicopter either an AugustaWestland Wildcat HMA2 or an Augusta Westland Merlin Mk2. These ships are designed to be very modular in design, so it is likely that they may be readily reconfigurable to match specific mission or deployment profiles.

On 20 January 2020, the Public Accounts Committee was informed by the Permanent Secretary for Defence that the first ship will be launched by 2023 but the in-service date will be in 2027. This contrasts to earlier statements that the in-service date would be in 2023.

On 19 May 2021 First Sea Lord Admiral Tony Radakin announced the names of the five ships of the class which will be known as the Inspiration Class. The names represent key themes and operations which will dominate and shape the Royal Navy and Royal Marines global mission in the future. FORMIDABLE will represent carrier operations; BULLDOG, the operational advantage in the North Atlantic; ACTIVE, the forward deployment of ships across the globe; VENTURER, the drive for technology and innovation and CAMPBELTOWN representing the Royal Marines new Future Commando Force.

The first steel for the lead Inspiration-class warship will be cut in the second half of 2021.

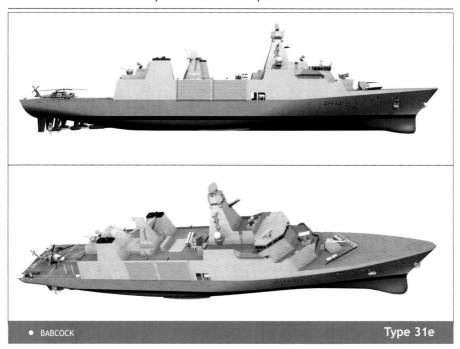

● BABCOCK   Type 31e

TYPE 32

With these ships Prime Minister Boris Johnson famously said he wanted to 'spur a shipbuilding renaissance' in the United Kingdom. Are these the warships to do this? The announcement of the Type 32 frigates came as something of a surprise to most naval analysts when first announced on 19 November 2020 as part of a defence investment pledge prior to the Integrated Review.

Where the Type 26 frigates will make up the high end of the technological mainstream of the fleet, Type 32s would be designed primarily to act in defence of the territorial or littoral waters around Great Britain and to provide 'persistent presence' in support of the new Littoral Response Groups (LRGs).

Much of the design work on the Type 32 has yet to be completed but what is known is that Defence Minister Ben Wallace envisages these ships to act as a 'platform for autonomous systems' and used in the widest variety of roles from anti-submarine warfare and mine countermeasures activities. They will also share a common heritage with the Type 26 and Type 31e in that they will be of modular design and general purpose in focus with the construction work expected to go to Scottish shipyards.

OCEAN SURVEILLANCE SHIP

One of the announcements made in 2021's Integrated Defence and Security Review was the planned construction of a dedicated Multi-Role Ocean Surveillance Ship (MROSS). This vessel will, it is hoped, be delivered to the Royal Navy by 2024 and will provide the fleet with the ability to undertake deep-sea surveillance of the critical undersea communication cables through which virtually all of the world's data and money transactions occur. Any break or sabotage to these vital links could be disastrous.

The new ship is expected to have a crew of around 15 and will be able to be deployed globally and particularly in the highly contested Arctic regions to conduct research, survey work and to provide command and control and support services to several smaller manned and unmanned autonomous undersea drones and other vessels currently planned to be joining the fleet over the next decade. Many of the new ship's functions are direct replacements for those found on SCOTT which will have been retired from service prior to the new ship's entry into service.

Defence Secretary Ben Wallace spoke of the new Ocean Surveillance Ship in Parliament: "As the threat changes, we must change. Our adversaries look to our critical national infrastructure as a key vulnerability and have developed capabilities that put these under threat. Some of our new investments will therefore go into ensuring that we have the right equipment to close-down these newer vulnerabilities. Whether on land, sea, or air, we must make sure that we maintain the UK resilience to those that attempt to weaken us."

TYPE 83 DESTROYERS

T he Integrated Defence Review highlighted the need to lay long-term ambitions to replace the current fleet of Type 45 Air Defence Destroyers in the late 2030 – early 2040 timeframe. Current thinking is to develop a version of the Type 26 frigate to perform this role originally known as the T4X project. 2021's Defence Command Paper stated that the United Kingdom will build a new class of warships with the aim being that 'the concept and assessment phase for our new Type 83 destroyer which will be begin to replace our Type 45 destroyers in the late 2030s'.

The use of a variant of a pre-existing design could prove to be a wise idea as it will cut design and development time and could create a continuous stream of shipbuilding in the United Kingdom for the Royal Navy. If the Royal Navy were to replace the Daring Class with six Type 83s, this could see the aim of continuous shipbuilding in Glasgow on the Type 26 production line extending beyond the eight Type 26s already ordered or projected.

ASTUTE CLASS SUCCESSOR - SSN(R)

I t is something of a truism in defence that you never stand still. Evolve or die. Such is the case with the development of attack submarines. In 2018 the Maritime Underwater Future Capability (MUFC) was established to determine the course of travel for future submarine development after the completion of the Astute class submarines. The MUFC was begun as an Initial Concept Phase but was almost immediately thereafter suspended for a further two years, most likely driven by the need to focus, time, money and energy into the Dreadnought and overrunning Astute programmes and get both back on track. Any other distractions from these two core projects it was assumed could be mitigated.

The MUFC resurfaced in the Integrated Defence Review and has the new name of SSN(R). With construction of the first of these submarines unlikely to commence much before the late 2030s, this project has a long way to run yet, but already there are some common threads that are likely to be incorporated into the new replacement submarine programme. Stealth technologies, both physical and technological and the growth in the use of unmanned systems will play an increasing part in the design philosophy.

It is extremely likely that the SS(R) will be up to 25 per cent larger than the Astutes they will replace to allow for the installation of a PWR-3 nuclear reactor, heavier armament and more defensive countermeasures. There is also the possibility that an enlarged 'hangar' for a Chalfont-type DDS may be incorporated into the design. An X tail is another consideration that respected industry analysts suspect are key drivers in the SSN(R)s current design.

A consideration for having larger submarines, however, would be the existing refit facilities at Devonport. The existing dry-docks would need to be extended to take the 25 per cent larger hull.

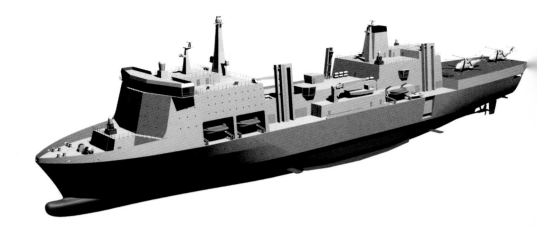

MILITARY AFLOAT REACH AND SUSTAINABILITY (MARS)

The long overdue contract for the construction of three Solid Support Ships under the MARS programme has, at the time of writing, yet to be placed with a shipbuilder. A great deal of the delay is due to political wrangling over semantics and the finer print of European Law, but with the United Kingdom's departure from the EU at the beginning of 2021 it was hoped that some clarity over the situation would prevail.

As of 21 October 2020, Defence Secretary Ben Wallace announced that the trio of Solid Support Ships would be built by 'British led teams' which raised the spectre of the contracts for the construction of these ships being awarded abroad, much to the consternation of UK shipyards, which have been arguing hard that the contracts for 'war like' vessels should remain within the United Kingdom.

The Solid Support Ships are vitally needed to replace positively geriatric 1970s built FORT AUSTIN and FORT ROSALIE which have been in reserve for many months awaiting final disposal and the 1992 built FORT VICTORIA. The new ships will be integrated with the UK Carrier Strike Groups.

A new competition to tender for the construction of the three Solid Support Ships was expected to be put out to tender earlier this year. Under the terms of the competition, international shipbuilders are invited to collaborate with UK companies, but a British firm must lead the successful bid. This does not however mean that final construction of the ships needs to take place within the UK, only that a significant proportion of the work does. As the contract for the three ships is likely to be in the region of £1.5 billion UK shipbuilders want to secure the contract within country but are likely to face stiff competition from Japan, Korea, Italy, and Spain. Each of the new ships proposed will have a total cargo capacity of up to 7000m squared, travel at speeds of up to 18 knots without resupply and be capable of undertaking underway replenishments-at-sea making headway of 12 knots. Each transferable load could weigh up to 5 tonnes and will used the advanced Replenishment-at-Sea Rig (HRAS) developed by Rolls Royce.

Royal Fleet Auxiliary

BAE SYSTEMS

RFA Wave Ruler

T raditionally, the Royal Fleet Auxiliary (RFA) has maintained its civilian manned status while still being owned by the Ministry of Defence. Their primary role is to supply the fuel, food, stores, and ammunition that sustain warships and their ship's companies whilst deployed. Their role is a crucial one and without the RFA the Royal Navy could not achieve its numerous operational roles and taskings globally. The RFA has, over the last five decades shrunk in line with the Royal Navy but has in recent years been seen as a 'force multiplier' standing in for a warship when one is unavailable or tasked elsewhere.

Frequently RFA ships have hit the headlines as the operating base for Royal Marine Commandos on drug smuggling smashing missions. By embarking anti-submarine helicopters these vessels offer a valuable extra hull to task group commanders.

TIDEFORCE, the last of four Tide-class tankers built in South Korea entered service in 2019. These vessels are the first new tankers since 2002 and are sorely needed. Now the focus shifts to the acquisition of Solid Stores Support Ships. This programme has been mired in controversy and false starts since its inception nearly two decades ago.

At the same time, the positively geriatric FORT ROSALIE and FORT AUSTIN are still, nominally at least, listed as active vessels, although neither has been for sea for many years. FORT VICTORIA, built in 1992, is also approaching her out of service date, but soldiers on.

The MARS replacement programme is a hot political potato that no one seems to want to kick, not even into the long grass where it seems to have found a resting place. But hot potatoes tend to start fires. A resolution to the MARS issue and where the ships are to be built should have been resolved by the end of 2021. The question remains, however, where they will be built, a) entirely in the UK; b) partially in the UK or c) built abroad. The last option will come with severe political fallout for Prime Minister Boris Johnson's re-election hopes in 2024/25 in British shipbuilding communities.

There also remains a question about ARGUS, the RFA's aviation support ship and nominal casualty reception vessel. She is scheduled to leave service within the next two years and there are currently no plans to replace her. Her flight deck is a valuable piece of training space for helicopter crews and her medical facilities are not replicated elsewhere in the fleet.

Ships	P. No.	Page	Ships	P. No.	Page
Tankers			Stores Ship/Tankers		
TIDESPRING	A136	81	FORT VICTORIA	A387	85
TIDERACE	A137	81			
TIDESURGE	A138	81	Amphibious Ships		
TIDEFORCE	A139	81			
WAVE KNIGHT	A389	80	LYME BAY	L3007	86
WAVE RULER	A390	80	MOUNTS BAY	L3008	86
			CARDIGAN BAY	L3009	86
Stores Ships					
			Primary Casualty Receiving		
FORT ROSALIE	A385	84	Ship/Aviation Training Ship		
FORT AUSTIN	A386	84			
			ARGUS	A135	89

● CROWN COPYRIGHT/MOD

RFA Wave Knight

FAST FLEET TANKERS
WAVE CLASS

Ship	Pennant Number	Completion Date	Builder
WAVE KNIGHT	A389	2002	BAE Systems
WAVE RULER	A390	2002	BAE Systems

Displacement: 31,500 tonnes (FL) **Dimensions:** 196.5m x 28.25m x 10m **Machinery:** Diesel-electric: 4 Wärtsilä DG, 25,514 hp (18.76 MW); 2 GEC Alstom motors with variable speed converters, 19,040 hp (14 MW); 1 shaft; 1 bow and stern thruster **Speed:** 18 knots **Armament:** 2 x Vulcan Phalanx, 2 x 30mm **Aircraft:** Up to 2 Merlin **Complement:** 80 (plus 22 Fleet Air Arm)

Notes: These two vessels have a displacement of 31,500 tonnes and are powered by diesel-electric propulsion. Each has three replenishment rigs on port and starboard and a Hudson reel-type system at the stern. Capacity is 16,900 tonnes of fuel and 915 tonnes of dry stores. They were designed with vertical replenishment with a large hangar and flight deck rated for two Merlin type helicopters. The ships have modern medical facilities and their reverse-osmosis equipment can produce 100m3 of drinkable water every day, making these vessels ideal for use in humanitarian missions, which they have been frequently in the past. In February 2020 WAVE KNIGHT returned to the United Kingdom having spent seven-months in the Middle East as a 'floating service station' for coalition warships east of Suez and NATO's security mission in the Mediterranean Operation Sea Guardian. During her time on mission WAVE KNIGHT fuelled 29 warships from America, Spain, France, and the United Kingdom pumping 12,276,000 litres of fuel, enough for 220,000 family cars. As of June 2020, WAVE RULER was reported to be in reduced readiness (reserve) but maintained in good condition and available for reactivation.

RFA Tiderace

FLEET TANKERS
TIDE CLASS

Ship	Pennant Number	Completion Date	Builder
TIDESPRING	A136	2017	Daewoo Shipbuilding
TIDERACE	A137	2018	Daewoo Shipbuilding
TIDESURGE	A138	2018	Daewoo Shipbuilding
TIDEFORCE	A139	2019	Daewoo Shipbuilding

Displacement: 39,000 tonnes (FL) **Dimensions:** 200.9m x 28.6m x 10m **Machinery:** 2 Wärtsilä diesels, 20,394 hp; 2 shafts **Speed:** 26.8 knots **Armament:** 2 x Phalanx CIWS; 2 x 30mm **Aircraft:** 1 x Merlin or Wildcat **Complement:** 63 (plus 26 spare berths)

Notes: At 39,000 tonnes displacement these four ships are the largest vessels operated by the Royal Fleet Auxiliary. They are based on a BMT Defence Services' design called AEGIR-26 and are double-hulled to prevent any oil spillage into the world's oceans through a ruptured hull. The Tide Class were designed in parallel with the QUEEN ELIZABETH class aircraft carriers and their replenishment rigs are compatible.

Each ship has three abeam RAS(L) stations, (one to port and two to starboard) for diesel oil, aviation fuel and fresh water. A typical RAS transfer weighs around 2 tonnes. The ships also have aviation facilities for the operation of a single Wildcat or Merlin helicopter which can be used for vertical replenishments. As of 2021 the planned fitting of stern fuel delivery systems has yet to be undertaken. Tide-class tankers can deliver 800 cubic metres of fuel an hour.

TIDESPRING underwent a maintenance refit at Cammell Laird's shipyard in Birkenhead in March 2019. The following year she was involved in the largest Royal Navy response to a fleet of Russian warships in the North Sea. In September 2020, TIDESPRING supported the frigate SUTHERLAND during exercises in the Barents Sea with warships from the navies of Denmark, Norway and the United States.

TIDERACE in June 2020 emerged from a refit at Cammell Laird in Birkenhead. In March 2021 she supported the Type 23 frigates LANCASTER and WESTMINSTER during Exercise Baltic Dash conducted in icy and stormy conditions. The exercise was a test of the UK led Expeditionary Force to work with Baltic nations especially Latvia, Estonia, and Lithuania.

TIDESURGE in January 2020 underwent a maintenance refit at Cammell Laird's shipyard.

In October 2020 TIDEFORCE joined up with other units assigned to the UK's Carrier Strike Group centred on QUEEN ELIZABETH. The Carrier Strike Group is the largest and most powerful European-led maritime force in over two decades. In 2021 TIDEFORCE and RFA FORT VICTORIA will provide all the fuel, ammunition and spare necessary to sustain the force operationally during the aircraft carrier's first major overseas deployment to the Indo Pacific region.

RFA Tidesurge (left), Fort Victoria and Tideforce

RFA Cardigan Bay

RFA Fort Rosalie

STORES VESSELS
FORT CLASS I

Ship	Pennant Number	Completion Date	Builder
FORT ROSALIE	A385	1978	Scott Lithgow
FORT AUSTIN	A386	1979	Scott Lithgow

Displacement: 23,384 tonnes **Dimensions:** 183m x 24.1m x 9m **Machinery:** 1 Sulzer 8-cylinder RND90 diesel, 22,300 shp; 1 shaft; 2 bow thrusters **Armament:** 2 x Phalanx CIWS **Speed:** 22 knots **Complement:** 201, (120 RFA, 36 MoD Civilians & 45 Fleet Air Arm)

Notes: The oldest members of the fleet having been designed and built in the early 1970s. At the time of their conception, the Fort I-class were ground-breaking with full hangar and maintenance facilities for up to four large naval helicopters, with landing spots on the flight deck and another atop the hangar roof. Each ship has six replenishment stations in addition to being able to use helicopters for vertical replenishment profiles. Both saw service in the Falklands War of 1982 and extensive service worldwide after that. However, their service careers are effectively at an end. Both ships have old and now obsolete replenishment rigs which make them incompatible with the replenishment systems employed aboard QUEEN ELIZABETH and PRINCE OF WALES, which would, under any normal, circumstances have been their primary naval customers.

The 2021 Strategic Defence and Security Review stated that both vessels would be decommissioned and are unlikely to see further service. Both are laid up at Birkenhead awaiting sale for demolition. They will probably be retained in reserve until the new Solid Support Ships are delivered, but this has yet to be confirmed.

RFA Fort Victoria

REPLENISHMENT SHIPS
FORT CLASS II

Ship	Pennant Number	Completion Date	Builder
FORT VICTORIA	A387	1992	Harland & Wolff

Displacement: 33,675 tonnes Dimensions: 204m x 30m x 9m Machinery: 2 Crossley-Pielstick V-16 diesels, 23,904 hp; 2 shafts Speed: 20 knots Armament: 2 x 30mm Oerlikon / BMARC KAA guns in GAM-B01 mounts, 2 x Phalanx CIWS, 15 cell Sea Wolf Missile System (fitted for but not with) Complement: 95 RFA, 24 MoD Civilians, 15 RN and up to 154 Fleet Air Arm

Notes: In the 1970s the logic of having one replenishment ship for fuel and another for solid supplies was being questioned. Such a profile created waste and an unnecessary line of potential targets for enemy attack to disrupt Royal Navy activities. In response a 'one stop shop' design was formulated that provided fuel, food, supplies, spares, and ammunition in just one hull. The result was a very expensive but extremely capable floating supermarket that can also operate as a mobile base of maritime operations. With a large hangar and flight deck this ship can operate up to 5 Wildcat or 3 Merlin Helicopters. Furthermore, FORT VICTORIA has a 12-bed medical facility that was upgraded in recent years with the latest medical equipment. FORT VICTORIA received a major upgrade to her systems and extra protection to her fuel tanks in a refit in 2018 carried out by Cammell Laird shipyard at Birkenhead. Early 2020 Cammell Laird completed the vessel's 30 year Special Survey that saw inspection and maintenance of the vessel's main engines, propulsion system and steering gear, a full tank survey was carried out and a new hangar crane installed. In 2021 FORT VICTORIA and a TIDE-class tanker will provide logistical support for the UK's Carrier Strike Group's first major overseas deployment to the Indo Pacific region.

RFA Mounts Bay

LANDING SHIP DOCK (AUXILIARY) BAY CLASS

Ship	Pennant Number	Completion Date	Builder
LYME BAY	L3007	2007	Swan Hunter
MOUNTS BAY	L3008	2006	BAE Systems
CARDIGAN BAY	L3009	2007	BAE Systems

Displacement: 16,190 tonnes **Dimensions:** 176.6m x 26.4m x 5.8m **Machinery:** Diesel-electric; 2 Wärtsilä 8L26 DG, 6,000 hp (4.5 MW); 2 × Wärtsilä 12V26 DG, 9,000 hp (6.7 MW); 2 azimuthing thrusters; 1 bow thruster **Speed:** 18 knots **Armament:** 2 x Phalanx CIWS (exact weapons fit varies within the class) **Complement:** 60

Notes: The three Bay-class amphibious landings ships can offload embarked troops and armoured vehicles from ship-to-shore using their onboard Landing Craft Vehicle Personnel (LCVP) and Landing Craft Utility (LCU) vessels. They are highly versatile and can operate in extremely rough weather to support amphibious operations and ground forces across the globe.

During last year's summer months, shiprepairer A&P Falmouth and its specialist division A&P Defence were busy working on two of the Royal Fleet Auxiliary's two Bay-class landing ship dock (auxiliary) vessels MOUNTS BAY and LYME BAY.

Following a three year deployment to the Caribbean as the UK's Atlantic Patrol Tasking North vessel, MOUNTS BAY arrived in Falmouth on 25 March 2020 to begin a major refit, work which included a five month stay in the yard's Queen Elizabeth graving dock.

The work package carried out on MOUNTS BAY was part of A&P Falmouth's 10-year FISS (Future In-Service Support) contract with the UK's Ministry of Defence (MOD). The scope of work includes repairs and maintenance to the vessel's main propulsion drive, main chilled water plant and sewage treatment plant, as well as work on the preservation and prevention of the ship's ballast water tanks. The vessel's galley was given a full upgrade, while the hull and superstructure of MOUNTS BAY was given a full back-to-bare-steel repainting.

LYME BAY returned to Falmouth on 15 May 2020 for a major Contractors Support Period. Work included the overhaul of the vessel's diesel-electric propulsion system plus the replacement of all resilient mounts on all engines, a large package of steel repairs on the cranes, cargo lifts and ramps, along with electrical work on the vessel's 6.6kV and 440V switchboards, plus repairs to the ship's bow thrusters motor.

CARDIGAN BAY is currently deployed to the Persian Gulf to serve as mother ship to the Royal Navy's minehunters and frigates in the region on Operation Kipion. In April 2021 MOUNTS BAY conducted training with US Air Force's 7th Special Operation Squadron who operate the Bell Boeing MV-22 Osprey tiltrotor.

LYME BAY in late 2020 operated in the Mediterranean with the assault ship ALBION and the Italian aircraft carrier GARIBALDI.

Under the terms of 2021's Integrated Defence and Security Review and the subsequent Defence Command Paper, one of the Bay Class will be converted to serve as a command ship for the Future Marine Force. The Review stated: "The Royal Navy will invest £40 million more over the next four years to develop our Future Commando Force as part of the transformation of our amphibious forces, as well as more than £50 million in converting a Bay-class support ship to deliver a more agile and lethal littoral strike capability."

"Forward deployed to respond rapidly to crises, this special operations capable force will operate alongside our allies and partners in areas of UK interest, ready to strike from the sea, pre-empt and deter sub threshold activity, and counter state threats. This will be enabled by the deployment of two Littoral Response Groups; the first in 2021 will be deployed to the Euro Atlantic under a NATO and JEF construct, while a second will be deployed to the Indo Pacific region in 2023. They will also be able to deliver training to our partners in regions of the world where maritime security is most challenging."

It has not yet been announced which of the three ships will be converted.

RFA Argus

RFA Argus

PRIMARY CASUALTY RECEIVING SHIP/ AVIATION TRAINING SHIP

Ship	Pennant Number	Completion Date	Builder
ARGUS	A135	1981	Cantieri Navali Breda

Displacement: 28,481 tonnes (Full Load) Dimensions: 175.1m x 30.4m x 8.1m
Machinery: 2 Lindholmen Pielstick 18 PC2.5V diesels, 23,400 hp; 2 shafts; 1 bow thruster
Speed: 18 knots Armament: 4 x 30mm, 2 x 20mm Aircraft: up to 6 Merlin
Complement: 254 (inc 137 FAA)

Notes: ARGUS is the United Kingdom's Primary Casualty Receiving/Aviation Training Ship in which capacity she operates an extensive Role 3 100 bed medical facility complete with CT scanner and radiology research and a dentistry operating theatre. The care facility operates with a staff of up to 250 doctors, nurses and support staff. As the ship is armed (2 × Oerlikon 20mm/85 KAA on GAM-BO1 mountings and 4 × 7.62mm GPMGs Mk44 Miniguns) and is not painted in the required white with red crosses, the Geneva Convention prevents her from being officially classified as a hospital ship.

Her aviation training role is crucial in allowing new naval helicopter pilots at sea experience of landing on the pitching and rolling deck at sea. Although the construction of a casualty access lift together with a new deckhouse aft of the superstructure has reduced helicopter capability by one landing spot.

However, currently ARGUS is scheduled to be withdrawn from service in 2024 without replacement because there are no firm plans on how to procure a replacement platform to undertake these roles.

The Ministry of Defence has left the question of her replacement outstanding stating that, "The considerations of options to deliver these capabilities after ARGUS leaves service remains ongoing." Those words were spoken in February 2020 and no further decision has been made since then.

ARGUS is an elderly ship having first been launched as a roll-on, roll-off ferry, and container ship in 1981. Taken up from Trade for the Falklands War of 1982 she was subsequently converted to act as an aviation ship replacing the ENGADINE. In 2009 she was further converted to provide the Royal Navy with its only Primary Casualty Receiving Ship. In the past her flexibility was proven when she was used to help fight an Ebola outbreak in West Africa, disaster relief missions in the Caribbean and during the First Gulf War of 1990 she was used as a hospital ship.

Some naval commentators believe that training of naval helicopter pilots at sea may have to be undertaken on either QUEEN ELIZABETH or PRINCE OF WALES, which would be a poor and uneconomic use of a valuable naval asset.

RFA Argus

MT Raleigh Fisher

COMMERCIAL TANKER

Ship	Completion Date	Builder
RALEIGH FISHER	2005	Guangzhou Shipyard, China

Displacement: 22,184 tonnes (GRT); 35,191 tonnes (DWT) Dimensions: 172m x 28m x 8.3m Machinery: 2SA 5 cylinder Burmeister & Wain diesel, 9,721 hp; 1 shaft; bow thruster Speed: 14.5 knots

Notes: In 2019 Maersk took their remaining vessels off the UK Ship Register, exiting the UK Tonnage Tax and ending the training of UK cadets, and sold the tanker MAERSK RALEIGH to UK-based James Fisher and Sons for £9 million.

Nick Henry, James Fisher chief executive, said that the renamed tanker - RALEIGH FISHER - would be significant for their tanker business as the vessel is presently contracted to the Ministry of Defence to support the Royal Navy's fuelling needs, both in the UK and abroad, on a five-year contract. The MoD charters the vessel to commercial companies when it is not in use for their own requirements.

RALEIGH FISHER is the ex ROSA MAERSK and was renamed and reflagged (to UK flag) in August 2017. She has taken over from MAERSK RAPIER which was sold in June 2017 to an unnamed party for USD6.5 million and renamed DOLICHA BAY.

RALEIGH FISHER will be used to move fuel products between the UK, the Falkland Islands and Cyprus, where the MoD supplies RAF Akrotiri with jet fuel. RAF Akrotiri is located on the southern tip of Cyprus and is the service's busiest base.

CROWN COPYRIGHT/MOD

MV Hartland Point

STRATEGIC SEALIFT RO-RO VESSELS
POINT CLASS

Ship	Pennant Number	Completion Date	Builder
HURST POINT		2002	Flensburger
HARTLAND POINT		2002	Harland & Wolff
EDDYSTONE		2002	Flensburger
ANVIL POINT		2003	Harland & Wolff

Displacement: 10,000 tonnes, 13,300 tonnes (FL) **Dimensions:** 193m x 26m x 7.6m
Machinery: 2 MaK 94M43 diesels, 21,700 hp; 2 shafts; 2 CP propellers; 1 bow thruster
Speed: 18 knots **Complement:** 18-22

Notes: Foreland Shipping Limited operated 6 Ro-Ro vessels built at yards in the UK and Germany under a Private Finance Initiative (PFI) deal which was signed with the MoD on 27 June 2002 and runs until 31 December 2024. While the current main focus is on transporting equipment to and from the Middle East/Gulf in support of military activities, the vessels also make regular voyages to the Falkland Islands, Canada and Norway in support of training exercises. Each vessel can carry 130 armoured vehicles and 60 trucks and ammunition or 8,000 tonnes of vehicles. There is 2,650 linear metres of space for vehicles. It can transport up to four helicopters including Chinook, Apache, Merlin and Wildcat. The ships are all named after English lighthouses. They come under the operational umbrella of Defence Supply Chain Operation and Movements (DSCOM), part of the Defence Logistics Organisation. In 2012 the requirement was reduced from six to four ships. BEACHY HEAD and LONGSTONE were subsequently sold.

Serco Marine Service

SD Tempest *assisting* **HMS Queen Elizabeth**

S erco Marine Services offers support to the Naval Service and the Royal Fleet Auxiliary in both port and deep-water operations including a wide range of waterborne and associated support activities, both in and out of port, at Portsmouth, Devonport and on the Clyde, as well as maintenance of UK and overseas moorings and navigational marks and support of a range of military operations and training. In-port services include the provision of berthing and towage activities within the three naval bases; passenger transportation, including pilot transfers and the transportation of stores, including liquids and munitions. The recovery and disposal of waste from ships and spillage prevention and clean-up also fall within their tasking. There is also a requirement for substantial out-of-port operations. Diving training, minelaying exercises, torpedo recovery, boarding training and target towing duties are also undertaken.

The support is all part of a £1 billion Private Finance Initiative (PFI) contract awarded by the MoD in December 2007 to Serco Denholm Marine Services Limited for the Future Provision of Marine Services (FPMS) for the next 15 years.

In 2009 Serco bought out Denholm's share and the SD funnel logos were replaced by a prominent Serco logo on the superstructure. All Serco Marine Services vessels carry the ship prefix SD.

The Briggs Group has been sub-contracted to assist with buoys and mooring support work. The ships KINGDOM OF FIFE and CAMERON are provided by Briggs Marine who won a £100M subcontract from Serco Marine Services for the support and maintenance of the Royal Navy's navigational marks (or buoys) and moorings in the United Kingdom and overseas. In February 2020 it was revealed that both companies teamed to bid for the Royal Navy's next generation of marine services, known as Marine Services 2022. The Marine Services 2022 contract will be the successor to the current Provision of Marine Services and Range Safety and Aircrew Training contracts held by the Ministry of Defence.

SHIPS OF SERCO MARINE SERVICES

Ship	Page	Ship	Page
SD ADEPT	100	SD OILMAN	115
SD ANGELINE	119	SD OMAGH	112
SD BOUNTIFUL	99	SD ORONSAY	112
SD BOVISAND	109	SD PADSTOW	111
SD CAREFUL	100	SD POWERFUL	100
SD CATHERINE	104	SD RAASAY	118
SD CAWSAND	109	SD RELIABLE	99
SD CHRISTINA	102	SD RESOURCEFUL	99
SD CLYDE RACER	120	SD SOLENT RACER	120
SD CLYDE SPIRIT	121	SD SOLENT SPIRIT	121
SD DEBORAH	102	SD SUZANNE	102
SD DEPENDABLE	99	SD TAMAR RACER	120
SD EILEEN	102	SD TAMAR SPIRIT	121
SD ENGINEER	118	SD TEESDALE	115
SD FAITHFUL	100	SD TEMPEST	97
SD FLORENCE	103	SD TILLY	105
SD FORCEFUL	100	SD VICTORIA	106
SD GENEVIEVE	103	SD WARDEN	107
SD HELEN	103	SD WATERPRESS	115
SD HERCULES	101		
SD IMPETUS	96		
SD IMPULSE	96	Briggs Sub-Contract	
SD INDEPENDENT	98		
SD INDULGENT	98	SD CAMERON	122
SD INSPECTOR	118	SD KINGDOM OF FIFE	122
SD JUPITER	101		
SD KYLE OF LOCHALSH	108	SMIT DEE	123
SD MARS	101	SMIT DART	123
SD MENAI	*114*	SMIT DON	123
SD MEON	*114*	SMIT YARE	123
SD MOORFOWL	117	SMIT SPEY	123
SD MOORHEN	117	SMIT STOUR	124
SD NAVIGATOR	118	SMIT ROTHER	124
SD NETLEY	110	SMIT ROMNEY	124
SD NEWHAVEN	110	SMIT CERNE	124
SD NORTHERN RIVER	116	SMIT FROME	124
SD NORTON	113	SMIT MERRION	124
SD NUTBOURNE	110	SMIT PENALLY	124
SD OBAN	112	SMIT WEY	124
SD OCEANSPRAY	115	SMIT NEYLAND	124

Entries displayed in lighter typeface have been removed from contract and are awaiting sale.

SD Impulse

TUGS

IMPULSE CLASS

Ship	Completion Date	Builder
SD IMPULSE	1993	Richard Dunston (Hull)
SD IMPETUS	1993	Richard Dunston (Hull)

G.R.T.: 319 tonnes **Dimensions:** 32.5m x 10.5m x 5.2m **Machinery:** 2 Allen 8S12 F-BC diesel engines; 3,400 hp; 2 Azimuth thrusters; 1 bow thruster **Speed:** 12 knots **Complement:** 5

Notes: Completed in 1993 specifically to serve as berthing tugs for the Trident-class submarines at Faslane. In February 2018 IMPULSE underwent a 25 year special survey in Garvel. Both her main engines underwent full overhaul as did both Aqua master propulsion units. Other work included the overhaul of the main forward and aft winches, all electrical and lifesaving equipment had annual checks and service and the ship's crane was serviced and load tested. Both are to be retained in service until 2022.

SD Tempest

ART 8032 CLASS

Ship	Completion Date	Builder
SD TEMPEST	2017	Damen (Poland)

G.R.T.: 495 tonnes **Dimensions:** 32.9m x 13.2m x 6.2m **Machinery:** 3 Caterpillar 3512C diesels, 5,295 kW; 3 Schottel SRP 1215 CP propellers **Speed:** 13 knots **Complement:** 4

Notes: SD Tempest has a bollard pull of 82 tonnes and is the most powerful tug in the fleet. Her primary role in Portsmouth is to support the Queen Elizabeth Class carriers although she will undertake other harbour towage work when not required in her primary role. She was ordered in February 2016 and launched in Gdansk (Poland) on 14 September 2016. In February 2017 she arrived at Portsmouth - her homeport. She is fitted with a foldable mast to allow her to operate under the flightdeck overhangs and is equipped with a double drum render/recovery aft winch.

SD Indulgent

ASD 2509 CLASS

Ship	Completion Date	Builder
SD INDEPENDENT	2009	Damen (Netherlands)
SD INDULGENT	2009	Damen (Netherlands)

G.R.T.: 345 tonnes approx   **Dimensions:** 25.14m x 9.44m x 4.45m   **Machinery:** 2 Caterpillar diesels; 3,500 hp; 2 RR thrusters; 1 bow thruster   **Speed:** 13 knots **Complement:** 4

Notes: Both INDEPENDENT and INDULGENT are classified as Azimuth Stern Drive (ASD) tugs with two azimuth thrusters under the stern. ASD tugs perform the majority of towing operations over the bow, from a winch mounted on the foredeck. Bollard pull is 40 tonnes. Both tugs are based at Portsmouth and are designed for coastal and harbour towage. They have been specifically modified for making cold moves within the Naval Base.

SD Bountiful

ATD 2909 CLASS

Ship	Completion Date	Builder
SD RELIABLE	2009	Damen (Netherlands)
SD BOUNTIFUL	2010	Damen (Netherlands)
SD RESOURCEFUL	2010	Damen (Netherlands)
SD DEPENDABLE	2010	Damen (Netherlands)

G.R.T.: 271 tonnes Dimensions: 29.14m x 9.98m x 4.41m Machinery: 2 Caterpillar diesels; 4,025 hp; 2 RR thrusters Speed: 13.1 knots Complement: 4 (Portsmouth); 5 (Clyde)

Notes: These Azimuthing Tractor Drive (ATD) tugs were built to a new design to provide assistance to warships and other vessels where exceptional manoeuvrability, precise control and adequate power are essential. Included in the design are a number of special features required specifically for use in the UK naval bases. Two double drum towing winches are fitted, along with extensive underwater fendering, fire fighting equipment and facilities for passenger and stores transportation. Construction of the hull and all major steel work for these vessels was undertaken by a Damen subsidiary in Poland. SD BOUNTIFUL is based at Portsmouth. SD RESOURCEFUL, SD RELIABLE and SD DEPENDABLE are based on the Clyde.

SD Careful

TWIN UNIT TRACTOR TUGS

Ship	Completion Date	Builder
SD ADEPT	1980	Richard Dunston
SD CAREFUL	1982	Richard Dunston
SD FAITHFUL	1985	Richard Dunston
SD FORCEFUL	1985	Richard Dunston
SD POWERFUL	1985	Richard Dunston

G.R.T.: 384 tonnes Dimensions: 38.8m x 9.42m x 4m Machinery: 2 Ruston diesels; 2,575 hp; 2 Voith-Schneider propellers Speed: 12 knots Complement: 5

Notes: These twin unit tractor tugs are the principal harbour tugs in naval service. All are based at Devonport and some are to undergo a service life extension programme.

Both SD FAITHFUL and SD POWERFUL were formerly operated by the Royal Maritime Auxiliary Service until its disbandment in March 2008.

SD Hercules

STAN TUG 2608 CLASS

Ship	Completion Date	Builder
SD HERCULES	2009	Damen (Netherlands)
SD JUPITER	2009	Damen (Netherlands)
SD MARS	2009	Damen (Netherlands)

G.R.T.: 133.92 tonnes **Dimensions:** 26.61m x 8.44m x 4.05m **Machinery:** 2 Caterpillar 3508B TA diesels; 2,200 hp; 2 Van de Giessen Optima nozzles; 90kW HRP hydraulically powered bow thruster **Speed:** 12 knots **Complement:** 4 (6 max)

Notes: The Stan Tug has proved to be a popular and versatile conventional twin-screw tug for coastal and port operations. For naval service the tug has a comprehensive outfit of equipment to fit it for a wide variety of tasks in addition to towage operations in port and at sea. Two towing winches are fitted, a combined anchor windlass and single drum winch is located on the foredeck and a double drum towing winch on the after deck. These tugs have a particularly spacious after deck particularly suitable for handling submarine mounted towed sonar arrays. Bollard pull of 29.5 tonnes. SD HERCULES is based at Devonport and SD JUPITER on the Clyde. SD MARS now at Kyle of Lochalsh replaced SD MELTON where she also provides passenger capability but with added value as a towage asset.

SD Deborah

ASD 2009 CLASS

Ship	Completion Date	Builder
SD CHRISTINA	2010	Damen (Poland)
SD DEBORAH	2010	Damen (Poland)
SD EILEEN	2010	Damen (Poland)
SD SUZANNE	2010	Damen (Poland)

G.R.T.: 120.74 tonnes Dimensions: 21.2m x 9.4m x 3.9m Machinery: 2 Caterpillar 3508B TA/C diesels; 2,000 hp; 2 Rolls Royce US 155CP thrusters Speed: 11 knots Complement: 5

Notes: These Azimuth Stern Drive (ASD) tugs are derived from the successful Damen ASD 2411 shiphandling tug with a bollard pull of 30 tonnes. Winches fore and aft, together with a bow thruster, make these tugs suitable for handling smaller surface ships, barge work and assisting with submarine movements. SD DEBORAH and SD EILEEN are based at Devonport, SD CHRISTINA and SD SUZANNE at Portsmouth.

SD Genevieve

FELICITY CLASS

Ship	Completion Date	Builder
SD FLORENCE	1980	Richard Dunston
SD GENEVIEVE	1980	Richard Dunston
SD HELEN	1974	Richard Dunston

G.R.T.: 88.96 tonnes   Dimensions: 22.0m x 6.4m x 2.6m   Machinery: 1 Mirrlees-Blackstone diesel; 615 hp; 1 Voith-Schneider CP propeller   Speed: 10 knots   Complement: 4 (Florence - 3)

Notes: The Felicity-class of water tractors (or tug boats) are used for the movement of small barges and equipment. They have a bollard pull of 5.7 tonnes. SD FLORENCE is based at Devonport with SD GENEVIEVE and SD HELEN at Portsmouth.

SD Catherine

PUSHY CAT 1204

Ship	Completion Date	Builder
SD CATHERINE	2008	Damen (Netherlands)

G.R.T.: 29.4 tonnes Dimensions: 12.3m x 4.13m x 1.55m Machinery: 1 Caterpillar diesel; 165 hp; 1 shaft Speed: 8 knots Complement: 2

Notes: Powered by a single Caterpillar 3056 TA diesel driving a single screw. A propulsion nozzle is fitted and twin rudders to give a 2.1 tonnes bollard pull. They are used as general line runner and harbour workboats. SD CATHERINE is based at Portsmouth.

SD Tilly

STAN TUG 1405

Ship	Completion Date	Builder
SD TILLY	2009	Damen (Netherlands)

G.R.T.: 45 tonnes Dimensions: 14.55m x 4.98m x 1.8m Machinery: 2 Caterpillar diesels; 600 hp; 2 Van de Giessen nozzles Speed: 9 knots Complement: 3

Notes: SD TILLY is a general purpose inshore and harbour tug based at Devonport. She is a general workboat, line handler and ideal for moving small barges.Effectively, she is a twin screw version of the Pushy Cat 1204 but slightly larger with a bow thruster and developing 8 tonnes of bollard pull.

● DEREK FOX

SD Victoria

WORLDWIDE SUPPORT VESSEL

Ship	Completion Date	Builder
SD VICTORIA	2010	Damen (Romania)

G.R.T.: 3,522 tonnes Dimensions: 83m x 16m x 4.5m Machinery: 2 Caterpillar diesels; 4,000 hp; 2 shafts; CP propellers; 1 bow thruster Speed: 14 knots Complement: 16 (accommodation for 72)

Notes: Built in Galatz (Romania) in 2010 the 83m training and support ship is the second largest vessel operated by Serco Marine Services in the UK and is based at Greenock's Great Harbour in Scotland. Powered by two Caterpillar 3516B diesels driving two shafts with controllable pitch propellers SD VICTORIA is designed to support training operations around the world. She is available for commercial charter and is primarily used to support military training and exercises as part of Serco's contract with the UK Ministry of Defence. She is equipped with classrooms, briefing rooms and operations rooms in addition to workshop facilities. There is provision to carry and operate RIBs and there is a helicopter winching deck.

SD Warden

TRIALS VESSEL

Ship	Completion Date	Builder
SD WARDEN	1989	Richards

Displacement: 626 tonnes Dimensions: 49m x 11m x 4m Machinery: 2 Ruston diesels; 4,000 hp; 2 shafts; CP propellers Speed: 15 knots Complement: 11

Notes: SD WARDEN was built in 1989 by Richards of Lowestoft as a Range Maintenance Vessel. She is based at Kyle of Lochalsh and functions as a Mooring and Weapons Recovery vessel owned and operated by Serco Marine and contracted to assist the Royal Navy. The harbour at Kyle of Lochalsh is a logistics base for vessels that support the work at the nearby British Underwater Test and Evaluation Centre (BUTEC) which is engaged in underwater weapons trials, sonar development and testing vessels noise signatures. She supports QinetiQ and the Royal Navy with experimental and trials work. She is the host vessel for Remotely Operated Vehicles (ROVs) and is also used to recover torpedoes. SD WARDEN is to remain in service until 2022.

SD Kyle of Lochalsh

TRIALS VESSEL

Ship	Completion Date	Builder
SD KYLE OF LOCHALSH	1997	Abels Boatbuilders

Displacement: 120 tonnes Dimensions: 24.35m x 9m x 3.45m Machinery: 2 Caterpillar diesels; 2,992 hp; 2 shafts Speed: 10.5 knots Complement: 4

Notes: The former twin-screw tug boat MCS LENIE was built in 1997 by Abels Boatbuilders in Bristol. She had been under contract to the MOD in Scotland for some time before she was purchased from Maritime Craft Services (Clyde) Ltd by Serco Marine Services and renamed SD KYLE OF LOCHALSH in 2008. She is used to support trials and operations at Kyle of Lochalsh. Bollard pull 26 tonnes.

RAYMOND WERGAN

SD Bovisand

TENDERS
STORM CLASS

Ship	Completion Date	Builder
SD BOVISAND	1997	FBM (Cowes)
SD CAWSAND	1997	FBM (Cowes)

G.R.T.: 225 tonnes Dimensions: 23m x 11m x 2m Machinery: 2 Caterpillar diesels; 1,224 hp; 2 shafts Speed: 15 knots Complement: 5

Notes: These tenders are used in support of Flag Officer Sea Training (FOST) at Plymouth to transfer staff quickly and comfortably to and from Warships and Auxiliaries within and beyond the Plymouth breakwater in open sea conditions. They were the first vessels of a Small Waterplane Area Twin Hull (SWATH) design ordered by the Ministry of Defence and cost £6.5 million each. Speed restrictions were implemented due to wash problems generated by these vessels. They are to remain in service until 2022.

SD Nutbourne

NEWHAVEN CLASS

Ship	Completion Date	Builder
SD NEWHAVEN	2000	Aluminium SB
SD NUTBOURNE	2000	Aluminium SB
SD NETLEY	2001	Aluminium SB

Displacement: 77 tonnes (45 grt) Dimensions: 18.3m x 6.8m x 1.88m Machinery: 2 Cummins diesels; 710 hp; 2 shafts Speed: 10 knots Complement: 2/3 Crew (60 passengers)

Notes: Employed on general passenger duties within the port area these MCA Class IV Passenger Vessels were acquired as replacements for Fleet tenders. SD NETLEY and SD NUTBOURNE are based at Portsmouth, SD NEWHAVEN is based at Devonport and operates in support of Flag Officer Sea Training (FOST). She has undergone modifications to strengthen her forward bollard and add transfer wings to enable underway personnel transfers with some classes of vessel undertaking sea training. They are all to remain in service until 2022.

SD Padstow

PADSTOW CLASS

Ship	Completion Date	Builder
SD PADSTOW	2000	Aluminium SB

Displacement: 77 tonnes (45 grt) **Dimensions:** 18.3m x 6.8m x 1.88m **Machinery:** 2 Cummins diesels; 710 hp; 2 shafts **Speed:** 10 knots **Complement:** 2/3 Crew (60 passengers)

Notes: SD PADSTOW was constructed by Aluminium Shipbuilders in Hampshire. The MCA Class IV, VI and VIA Passenger Vessel is based at Devonport. Used on liberty runs in Plymouth Sound and the Harbour as well as occasionally supporting FOST. She has undergone similar modifications as SD NEWHAVEN (see previous page) in order to conduct underway personnel transfers. She is to remain in service until 2022.

SD Oban

OBAN CLASS

Ship	Completion Date	Builder
SD OBAN	2000	McTay Marine
SD ORONSAY	2000	McTay Marine
SD OMAGH	2000	McTay Marine

G.R.T.: 199 tonnes Dimensions: 27.7m x 7.30m x 3.75m Machinery: 2 Cummins diesels; 1,050 hp; 2 Kort-nozzles Speed: 10 knots Complement: 4 Crew (60 passengers)

Notes: The three Oban-class tenders (MCA Class IIA Passenger Vessels) replaced the Fleet tenders in 2001. The lead ship of the class, SD OBAN, was originally based on the Clyde but was transferred to Devonport in 2003 and is now primarily used to support FOST staff. The other two, SD ORONSAY and SD OMAGH are employed on general passenger duties on the Clyde and are additionally classified as Cargo Ship VIII(A). All three are to remain in service until 2022.

PERSONNEL FERRY

Ship	Completion Date	Builder
SD NORTON	1989	FBM Marine

G.R.T.: 21 tonnes Dimensions: 15.8m x 5.5m x 1.5m Machinery: 2 Mermaid Turbo diesels; 280 hp; 2 shafts Speed: 13 knots Complement: 2

Notes: SD NORTON is a single FBM catamaran, 8837, operating at Portsmouth. She can carry 30 passengers or 2 tonnes of stores. She was designed as a prototype personnel launch catamaran designed to replace older Harbour Launches but no more were ordered.

SD Menai

FLEET TENDERS

Ship	Completion Date	Builder
SD MENAI	1981	Richard Dunston
SD MEON	1982	Richard Dunston

G.R.T.: 117.3 tonnes **Dimensions:** 24m x 6.7m x 3.05m **Machinery:** 1 Lister Blackstone diesel; 320 hp; 1 shaft **Speed:** 10.5 knots **Complement:** 4 (12 passengers)

Notes: The last two survivors of a once numerous class of vessels used as Training Tenders, Passenger Ferries or Cargo Vessels are now laid up in Devonport. Both SD MENAI and SD MEON are currently up for sale and a vessel replacement programme seems unlikely. SD MELTON was already released from contract and put up for sale. Her role has been taken over by SD MARS. In March 2019, SD MELTON was acquired by Edinburgh-based medical-oriented charity Vine Trust which intends to operate her as a medical vessel complete with consultation rooms, a dental clinic, an operating room, a laboratory and a pharmacy. Over the next 12 to 18 months she is set to undergo conversion work prior to being deployed on medical missions overseas.

SD Teesdale

COASTAL OILER

Ship	Completion Date	Builder
SD TEESDALE	1976	Yorkshire Drydock Co.

G.R.T.: 499 tonnes Dimensions: 43.86m x 9.5m x 3.92m Speed: 8 knots Complement: 5

Notes: SD TEESDALE was formerly the oil products tanker TEESDALE H operated by John H Whitaker. She operates as a parcel tanker delivering diesel and aviation fuel and also delivering/receiving compensating water. She is self-propelled by two Aquamaster thrusters. A Diesel Lighter Barge, SD OILMAN, and a Water Lighter Barge, SD WATERPRESS, are operated on the Clyde. A further barge, SD OCEANSPRAY, a Liquid Mixed Lighter Barge, is based at Portsmouth.

MULTI-PURPOSE VESSEL

Ship	Completion Date	Builder
SD NORTHERN RIVER	1998	Myklebust (Norway)

G.R.T.: 3,605 tonnes Dimensions: 92.8m x 18.8m x 4.9m Machinery: 2 Bergen diesels; 9,598 hp; 2 shafts; CP propellers; 2 bow thrusters Speed: 14 knots Complement: 14

Notes: SD NORTHERN RIVER is currently the largest multi-purpose auxiliary ship operated by Serco Marine Services, both in terms of dimensions and gross tonnage. She was bought from Deep Ocean AS (a subsidiary of Trico Marine). The Ulstein UT-745L designed Support Vessel entered service with Serco in March 2012. She can be employed on a variety of tasking from target towing, through noise ranging to data gathering; boarding training to submarine escort. Her extensive flat work deck allows her to embark containers for passive sonar training. She can also provide nuclear emergency support as well as support to submarine emergencies. She can provide mother ship training facilities for the NATO Submarine Rescue System (NSRS), which involves the embarkation, fitting and operation of specialist ROV's, escape vessels and Transfer Under Pressure (TUP) facilities on the after deck, together with the embarkation of up to 40 additional personnel. She can also support the Submarine Parachute Assistance Group.

SD Moorfowl

DIVING SUPPORT VESSELS
MOOR CLASS

Ship	Completion Date	Builder
SD MOORFOWL	1989	McTay Marine
SD MOORHEN	1989	McTay Marine

Displacement: 518 tonnes **Dimensions:** 36m x 12m x 2m **Machinery:** 2 Cummins diesels; 796 hp; 2 Aquamasters; 1 bow thruster **Speed:** 8 knots **Complement:** 10

Notes: Designed as a powered mooring lighter for use within sheltered coastal waters the lifting horns have been removed from the bows of both vessels when they were converted to Diving Support Vessels. They are used by the Defence Diving School for diving training in the Kyle of Lochalsh. In January 2016 SD MOORHEN had a main engine and generator overhaul. During this time, the Aquamaster propulsion unit was also overhauled, which involved removing the port unit for work at Rolls Royce. She also had a hull UT survey, steelwork repairs, HP wash and paint were carried out and her tank was cleaned, coated and certified to finish. Both vessels are to remain in service until 2022.

SD Navigator

MULTICAT 2510 CLASS

Ship	Completion Date	Builder
SD NAVIGATOR	2009	Damen (Netherlands)
SD RAASAY	2010	Damen (Netherlands)

Displacement: 362 tonnes **Dimensions:** 25.54m x 10.64m x 2.34m **Machinery:** 2 Caterpillar diesels; 957 hp; 2 shafts **Speed:** 8.4 knots **Complement:** 3 (plus up to 12 additional personnel)

Notes: SD NAVIGATOR is equipped for buoy handling with a single 9 tonnes capacity crane. She is capable of supporting diving operations. SD NAVIGATOR is managed from Devonport but operates between Devonport and Portsmouth. SD RAASAY is based at the Kyle of Lochalsh and is fitted with two cranes for torpedo recovery and support diving training. Two similar, but smaller vessels, SD INSPECTOR (ex-DMS EAGLE until March 2003 and ex-FORTH INSPECTOR until December 2007) and SD ENGINEER, operate from Portsmouth and Devonport respectively. SD INSPECTOR is a Utility Vessel that was built in 2001 with a length overall of 18.7m and width of 8m. SD ENGINEER is a Work Vessel that was built in 1996 with a length overall of 17.49m and width of 8.06m.

SD Angeline

MULTICAT 2613 CLASS

Ship	Completion Date	Builder
SD ANGELINE	2015	Damen (Netherlands)

Displacement: 657 tonnes Dimensions: 25.5m x 13.6m x 4m Machinery: 2 Caterpillar C32 TTA diesels; 2 Promarin fixed pitch propellers; bow thruster Speed: 10.1 knots Complement: Accommodation for 8 persons, consisting of four double crew cabins

Notes: SD ANGELINE was ordered in April 2014 and was accepted by the MoD in April 2015. Built at the request of the MoD to provide support in Faslane Naval Base primarily to submarines, but can undertake other naval base work. Her total power output is 2,850 kW with a bollard pull of 30.8 tonnes. The installed crane has a capacity of 15 tonnes.

SD Solent Racer

STAN TENDER 1505 CLASS

Ship	Completion Date	Builder
SD CLYDE RACER	2008	Damen (Netherlands)
SD SOLENT RACER	2008	Damen (Netherlands)
SD TAMAR RACER	2008	Damen (Netherlands)

G.R.T.: 25.19 tonnes **Dimensions:** 15.2m x 4.8m x 1.25m **Machinery:** 2 Caterpillar diesels; 1,100 hp; 2 shafts **Speed:** 26 knots **Complement:** 2 (+ 8 Passengers)

Notes: Fast twin-screw workboat made from an aluminium construction. These boats are employed on transfer of pilots, port security operations and VIP and passenger transportation.

● DEREK FOX

STAN TENDER 1905 CLASS

Ship	Completion Date	Builder
SD CLYDE SPIRIT	2008	Damen (Netherlands)
SD SOLENT SPIRIT	2008	Damen (Netherlands)
SD TAMAR SPIRIT	2008	Damen (Netherlands)

G.R.T.: 43.3 tonnes   Dimensions: 19.2m x 5.3m x 1.8m   Machinery: 2 Caterpillar diesels; 2,200 hp; 2 shafts   Speed: 25 knots   Complement: 2 (+ 10 passengers)

Notes: Steel hull with aluminium superstructure. Special propeller tunnels are fitted to increase propulsion efficiency and to reduce vibration and noise levels. These vessels are able to operate safely and keep good performance in wind speeds up to Force 6 and wave heights of 2 metres. Employed on transfer of pilots, VIPs and personnel.

SD Kingdom of Fife

ANCHOR HANDLING TUG

Ship	Completion Date	Builder
KINGDOM OF FIFE	2008	Damen (Romania)

Displacement: 1,459 tonnes Dimensions: 61.2m x 13.5m x 4.75m Machinery: 2 Caterpillar diesels, 2,720 hp each; 1 shaft; bow thruster Speed: 13.7 knots Complement: 18

Notes: Briggs Marine won a £100m contract from Serco to support navigation buoy maintenance and mooring support for the Royal Navy for 15 years. During the contract period, Briggs Marine provide support to Serco for a proportion of the 350 moorings, navigation buoys and targets for the RN all around the UK coast, as well as Cyprus, Gibraltar and the Falkland Islands. KINGDOM OF FIFE was delivered in May 2008 and supports the existing Briggs Marine shallow draught and heavy lift craft CAMERON in servicing the contract and can be equipped with a decompression chamber with support from the Serco dive team.

● LEE HARRISON

SD Cameron

Smit Dart

AIRCREW TRAINING VESSELS

Ship	Comp Date	Builder	Base Port
SMIT DEE	2003	BES Rosyth	Buckie
SMIT DART	2003	BES Rosyth	Plymouth
SMIT DON	2003	BES Rosyth	Blyth
SMIT YARE	2003	FBMA Cebu	Great Yarmouth
SMIT SPEY	2003	FBMA Cebu	Plymouth

G.R.T.: 95.86 GRT Dimensions: 27.6m x 6.6m x 1.5m Machinery: 2 Cummins diesels; 1,400 hp; 2 shafts; 1 centreline waterjet; 305hp Speed: 20 knots Complement: 6

Notes: The service for Marine Support to Range Safety and Aircrew Training is provided by SMIT International (Scotland) Ltd. A new seven year contract for £39m started in April 2018 and will run for five years until March 2023, with an option to extend for a further two years. These vessels provide support to aircrew training such as sea survival drills, various helicopter exercises, target towing and other general marine support tasks. They also participate in Navy Command sea training serials, particularly boarding exercises and force protection exercises involving fast attack craft scenarios. SMIT DART completed as a passenger vessel with a larger superstructure.

RANGE SAFETY VESSELS

Ship	Comp Date	Builder
SMIT STOUR	2003	Maritime Partners Norway
SMIT ROTHER	2003	Maritime Partners Norway
SMIT ROMNEY	2003	Maritime Partners Norway
SMIT CERNE	2003	Maritime Partners Norway
SMIT FROME	2003	Maritime Partners Norway
SMIT MERRION	2003	Maritime Partners Norway
SMIT PENALLY	2003	Maritime Partners Norway
SMIT WEY	2003	Maritime Partners Norway
SMIT NEYLAND	2003	Maritime Partners Norway

G.R.T.: 7.0 GRT   Dimensions: 12.3m x 2.83m x 0.89m   Machinery: 2 Volvo Penta diesels; 680 hp; 2 Hamilton waterjets Speed: 28 knots Complement: 2

Notes: A class of 12m Fast Patrol Craft which provide a range safety service to 7 land based ranges across the UK. They also participate in Navy Command Sea Training serials including participation in Fast Attack Craft scenarios. Part of a £39 million contract the MoD awarded to SMIT International (Scotland) Ltd in April 2018.

MATTHEW MCKIE

ARMY VESSELS
WORK BOATS

Vessel	Pennant Number	Completion Date	Builder
STORM	WB41	2008	Warbreck Eng.
DIABLO	WB42	2008	Warbreck Eng.
MISTRAL	WB43	2008	Warbreck Eng.
SIROCCO	WB44	2008	Warbreck Eng.

Displacement: 48 tonnes Dimensions: 14.75m x 4.30m Machinery: 2 John Deere Diesels; 402 hp; 2 shafts Speed: 10 knots Complement: 4

Notes: These work boats are part of the Army's strategic port operations in Southampton, but can be transported by a 'mother ship' to other ports and places like Iraq. Are often used as tugs for Mexeflotes, positioning other pontoon equipment and for handling flexible pipelines. They have a firefighting capability. The Army also operate a number of smaller Combat Support Boats. Built by RTK Marine/VT Halmatic (now BAE) these are fast and rugged small craft, 8.8m long with a twin Hamilton waterjet propulsion system powered by twin 210 hp diesel engines.

HMC Searcher

BORDER FORCE
STAN PATROL 4207 CLASS

Vessel	Callsign	Completion Date	Builder
SEARCHER	ZQNK9	2002	Damen
SEEKER	ZQNL2	2001	Damen
VALIANT	MBLL8	2004	Damen
VIGILANT	ZITI4	2003	Damen

G.R.T.: 238 tonnes Dimensions: 42.8m x 7.11m x 2.52m Machinery: 2 Caterpillar 3516B diesels, 2 shafts; 2 4-blade controllable pitch propellers; 1 Promac bow thruster Speed: 26+ knots Complement: 12

Notes: These vessels are able to remain at sea for extended periods and in heavy weather conditions. They are mostly deployed on a risk-led or intelligence-led basis detecting prohibited and restricted goods, boarding and searching ships and providing a law enforcement presence in remote and inaccessible areas. Vessels are prefixed HMC for Her Majesty's Cutter. They were built at the Damen Shipyard in the Netherlands and all have a steel hull with an aluminium superstructure.All are based at Portsmouth and are normally not armed with fixed firearms, nor are crew armed. What is often taken to be a gun on the bow of the cutters is in fact a water hose. A 7m rigid inflatable boat (RIB) can be launched from the stern slipway.

M FLOCH   HMC Protector

TELKKÄ CLASS

Vessel	Callsign	Completion Date	Builder
PROTECTOR	2GWY9	2002	UKI Workboat

Displacement: 434 tonnes **Dimensions:** 49.7m x 7.3m x 3.65m **Machinery:** 2 Wärtsilä 12V200 diesels, 7,240 hp; 2 shafts; CP propeller; bow and stern thrusters **Speed:** 22 knots **Complement:** 12

Notes: HMC PROTECTOR (not to be confused with HMS PROTECTOR) was acquired in August 2013 and commissioned in March 2014. She is the former Finnish Border Agency vessel TAVI. She replaced HMC SENTINEL which was retired in 2013. All HMC cutters operate 24 hours a day, 365 days per year, through the employment of dual crews. There are ten crews for the five Border Force cutters comprising 120 seagoing staff, working two weeks on and two weeks off.

● DEREK FOX

HMC Eagle

DELTA ARRC 190 CLASS

Vessel	Callsign	Completion Date	Builder
EAGLE	ZCPH5	2006	Holyhead Marine/Delta ARCC
NIMROD	2JQP9	2006	Holyhead Marine/Delta ARCC
ALERT	2JQQ2	2006	Holyhead Marine/Delta ARCC
ACTIVE	2JQQ3	2006	Holyhead Marine/Delta ARCC
HUNTER	ZCOO3	2006	Holyhead Marine/Delta ARCC
SPEEDWELL		2006	Holyhead Marine/Delta ARCC
ASTUTE		2006	Holyhead Marine/Delta ARCC
ARDENT		2006	Holyhead Marine/Delta ARCC

Displacement: 29 GRT **Dimensions:** 17.75m x 5.63m x 0.9m **Machinery:** 2 Caterpillar C18 diesels, 1,727 hp; 2 Hamilton waterjets **Speed:** 34 knots **Complement:** 6

Notes: Starting in 2016, to boost the number of vessels patrolling the UK coastline, eight ex-BP Project Jigsaw rescue craft, built by Holyhead Marine (Holyhead) and Delta ARCC (Stockport), were acquired by Border Force. They are termed Coastal Patrol Vessels within Border Force. As well as carrying out regular patrols of UK waters, CPVs will act on intelligence provided by law enforcement and international partners. Callsigns are displayed on superstructure roof forward of the bridge. The design includes a deep-vee fibre-reinforced plastic hull design and can return to the upright position if capsized.

AIRCRAFT & UNITS

NAVY COMMAND SQUADRONS

814 NAS*	Merlin HM2	TAG/RNAS Culdrose
815 NAS	Wildcat HMA2	Flights/RNAS Yeovilton
820 NAS	Merlin HM2	TAG/RNAS Culdrose
824 NAS	Merlin HM2	Training/RNAS Culdrose
825 NAS	Wildcat HMA2	Training/RNAS Yeovilton
849 NAS	Merlin HM2 'Crowsnest'	TAG/RNAS Culdrose
	Sea King ASaC7	Retired
727 NAS	Tutor T1	Grading/RNAS Yeovilton
736 NAS	Hawk T1	FOST/RNAS Culdrose
FOST Flight	Dauphin 2	HMNB Devonport

JOINT FORCE LIGHTNING

17 Sqn	F-35B Lightning II	Edwards AFB - USA
617 Sqn	F-35B Lightning II	TAG/RAF Marham
207 Sqn	F-35B Lightning II (projected)	Training/RAF Marham

JOINT HELICOPTER COMMAND

845 NAS	Merlin HC4/3i	TAG/RNAS Yeovilton
846 NAS	Merlin HC4/3i	TAG/RNAS Yeovilton
847 NAS	Wildcat AH1	TAG/RNAS Yeovilton
7 Sqn	Chinook HC4/4A/5	TAG/RAF Odiham
18 Sqn	Chinook HC4/4A/5	TAG/RAF Odiham
27 Sqn	Chinook HC4/4A/5	TAG/RAF Odiham
28(AC) Sqn	Chinook HC4/4A/5	Training/RAF Odiham
1 Regt.	Wildcat AH1	TAG/RNAS Yeovilton
3 Regt.	Apache AH1	TAG/AAC Wattisham
4 Regt.	Apache AH1	TAG/AAC Wattisham

MILITARY FLYING TRAINING SYSTEM

4(R) Sqn	Hawk T2	4 FTS/RAF Valley
72(R) Sqn	Tucano T1	1 FTS/RAF Linton-on-Ouse
703 Sqn	Tutor T1	3 FTS/RAF Barkston Heath
750 NAS	Avenger T1	RNAS Culdrose
705 Sqn	Juno HT1	DHFS/RAF Shawbury

*At the end of March 2018 829 Naval Air Squadron decommissioned and merged with 814 NAS.

CROWN COPYRIGHT/MOD

Leonardo Helicopters MERLIN HM2

Role: Anti-submarine search and strike; maritime surveillance
Engines: 3 x Rolls Royce/Turbomeca RTM 322 each developing 2,100 shp
Length: 74' 10" **Rotor:** diameter 61' **Height:** 21' 10"
Max. Weight: 32,120lb **Max. Speed:** 167 knots **Crew:** 1/2 pilots, 1 observer, 1 aircrewman
Avionics: Blue Kestrel radar; Orange Reaper ESM; Folding Light Acoustic System for helicopters (FLASH); AQS-903 acoustic processor; Wescam MX-15 electro-optical/IR camera; defensive aids including Directional Infrared Countermeasures (DIRCM), AN/AAR-57 radar warning system, chaff and flare dispensers;
Armament: Up to 4 Stingray torpedoes or Mark 11 depth charges; 1 x M3M 0.5" machine-gun in cabin door and 1 x 7.62mm machine-gun in cabin window

Squadron Service: 814, 820, 824, 849 Naval Air Squadrons

Notes: 814 NAS is the biggest Merlin Mk2 helicopter Squadron that the Royal Navy ever had (it merged with the decommissioned 829 Naval Air Squadron at the end of March 2018). The merger might signal the start of the execution of the MoD forward plan which shows 820 NAS allocated for carrier embarkation between 2018-2026 and 814 (and now 829) NAS specialising in providing aircraft for RFAs and frigates. 824 NAS is the training unit for all anti-submarine aircrew, ASaC 'Crowsnest' and commando Merlin pilots. 'Crowsnest' fitted Merlins in which anti-submarine role equipment can be replaced by ASaC sensors and consoles are being delivered by Leonardo helicopters. ASaC observer training will be carried out by the HQ Flight of 849 NAS and operational aircraft will be allocated to TAGs from 2021. The Merlin Mk2, as part of the the Crowsnest programme, has replaced the Navy's Sea King Mk7 Airborne Surveillance and Control of 849 Naval Air Squadron (now retired) – and like their predecessors will be based at Royal Naval Air Station Culdrose, which also provides anti-submarine Merlin aircraft to protect the Fleet.

NAVY COMMAND

Leonardo Helicopters WILDCAT HMA2

Roles: Surface search and strike; anti-submarine strike; boarding party support
Engines: 2 x LHTEC CTS 800 each developing 1,362 shp
Length: 50' **Rotor diameter:** 42' **Height:** 12'
Max. Weight: 13,200lb **Max. Speed:** 157 knots **Crew:** 1 pilot & 1 observer
Avionics: Selex-Galileo Sea Spray 7400E multi-mode AESA radar; Wescam MX-15 electro-optical/IR camera; Electronic warfare system and defensive aids suite. Bowman communications system
Armament: 2 x Stingray torpedoes or Mark 11 depth charges; 1 x M3M 0.5" machine-gun in cabin door. From 2020 to carry Martlet (light) and Sea Venom (heavy) air-to-surface guided weapons.

Squadron Service: 815, 825 Naval Air Squadrons

Notes: 825 NAS is the training and tactical development unit and 815 NAS deploys flights of 1 or 2 aircraft to destroyers, frigates and some RFAs that do not embark Merlins. Wildcat is designed around a digital avionics management system that enhances mission effectiveness and reduces aircrew workload. Its 'paperless' maintenance system is shared with the Wildcat AH 1 operated by the Joint Helicopter Command. With the Lynx HMA 8 withdrawn from service in 2017, Wildcats now fully equip these two naval air squadrons which are both shore-based at RNAS Yeovilton. The HMA 2 has a significant strike capability since the Martlet and Sea Venom air-to-surface guided weapons achieved initial operational capability. Each Wildcat helicopter is capable of carrying 20 Martlett missiles. With the withdrawal from service of 700X NAS ScanEagle detachments in 2017, Wildcats and Merlins are the only air assets capable of deployment in destroyers, frigates and RFAs.

BAE Systems HAWK T1

Role: Threat simulation aircraft
Engine: 1 x Rolls Royce Adour 151 delivering 5,200lb of thrust.
Length: 40' 9" Wingspan: 32' 7" Height: 13' 1"
Max. Weight: 20,000lb Max. Speed: Mach 0.88 (Mach 1.2 in a dive) Crew: 1 or 2 pilots
Avionics: standard communications fit
Armament: Can be fitted with a 30mm gun pod on a centreline pylon and one pylon under each wing capable of taking AIM-9 Sidewinder or up to 1,500lb of practice weapons

Squadron Service: 736 Naval Air Squadron

Notes: 736 NAS (the Royal Navy's 'maritime agressor squadron') is the focal point for fixed-wing flying standards and practices within the Navy Command structure and provides continuity flying for pilots destined to be fed into the F-35B Lightning II training programme. It also provides aircraft for fighter controller and ASaC observer training plus attack simulations for FOST activities and 'Joint Warrior' exercises, effectively acting as an RN 'aggressor unit'. The aircraft are maintained by Babcock, regularly operated from both RN Air Stations Culdrose and Yeovilton and frequently deploy in support of exercises and fleet deployments. Under current plans 736 NAS' Hawk T1s are due to be withdrawn from service in 2020 although T1s operated by Air Command, including those flown by the Red Arrows display team, are expected to run on for longer. In February 2019, 736 NAS took delivery of a new simulator – which replicates Hawk, Typhoon and F-35 cockpits – which can be used to recreate anything a pilot might encounter, from pulling extreme G forces to evading incoming missiles. An air-accident in March 2021 might accelerate plans to retire the Hawk T1s.

Grob TUTOR T1

Role: Elementary training
Engine: 1 x Textron Lycoming AE10-360-B1F developing 180 hp
Length: 24' 9" Wingspan: 32' 9" Height: 7'
Max. Weight: 2,178lb Max. Speed: 185 knots Crew: 2 pilots
Avionics: None
Armament: None

Squadron Service: 727 Naval Air Squadron, 703 Squadron MFTS

Notes: Tutors are used within Navy Command for the grading of potential aircrew and, in the short term, to clear a backlog in the MFTS. They provide elementary flying training for up to 12 student pilots per year. 703 Squadron is not a naval air squadron although it is numbered in what was until recently an exclusively naval sequence. It is part of the MFTS, providing elementary pilot training at RAF Barkston Heath for RN and RM pilots and Phase 1 and 2 training for RN observers. The aircraft is constructed mainly from carbon fibre reinforced plastic, which combines high strength with light weight. It has side-by-side seating with the primary flight instruments on the right-hand side of the cockpit.Thus the student flies the aircraft from the right-hand seat with a right-hand stick and a left-hand throttle making transition to operational aircraft easier.

Lockheed Martin F-35B LIGHTNING II

Role: Strike, fighter and reconnaissance aircraft
Engine: 1 X Pratt & Whitney F135-PW-600 delivering 41,000lb thrust with reheat in conventional flight; 40,650lb hover thrust with Rolls-Royce lift fan engaged and tail nozzle rotated.
Length: 51' 4"   **Wingspan:** 35'   **Height:** 15'
Max. Weight: 60,000lb **Max. Speed:** Mach 1.6 **Crew:** 1 pilot
Avionics: AN/APG-81 AESA radar; AN/AAQ-40 electro-optical targeting system; AN/AAQ-37 distributed aperture system; AN/ASQ-239 'Barracuda' electronic warfare system; pilot's helmet-mounted display system; multi-function advanced data link.
Armament: Current Block 2B software allows the stealthy carriage of weapons in 2 internal bays with a single ASRAAM or AMRAAM air-to-air missile plus a single 1,000lb bomb equivalent such as Paveway IV LGB in each. Block 3F software in operational aircraft delivered from 2017 will enable the additional use of 7 non-stealthy external pylons, 3 under each wing and 1 under the centreline. A total of 12,000lb of weapons or fuel tanks to be carried; inner wing pylons have 'plumbing' for 426 US gallon drop tanks.

Squadron Service: 17, 207, 617 Squadrons.

Notes: The F-35 is an Anglo-American joint effort with numerous British companies being part of the construction process. Around 25,000 British jobs are involved in the project and it is estimated that around £35 billion will be contributed to the UK economy. The UK has committed to purchase a total of 138 F-35B Lightnings II from Lockheed Martin over the life of the programme which will be ordered/delivered in batches. Forty-eight have been ordered and as of April 2020, the MoD had taken delivery of 18. The number of jets to be delivered will be three in 2020, six in 2021, eight in 2022, two in 2023, four in 2024 and seven in 2025. By 2025, the full 48 will have been delivered. However, this is misleading because that figure includes three test aircraft which will never leave the USA. This basically means that the Navy/RAF will only ever have 45 jets. The F-35B is

JOINT FORCE LIGHTNING

jointly operated by pilots from the Fleet Air Arm and the Royal Air Force.

809 Naval Air Squadron (NAS) has been resurrected as the first RN formation to operate the fifth generation stealth aircraft and will fly off the Royal Navy's Queen Elizabeth Class carriers. According to the RN, 809 Naval Air Squadron was selected because of its history of striking at the enemy in operations across the globe. In previous incarnations, aircraft from 809 supported an attack on Hitler's flagship, supported the invasions of North Africa, Italy and southern France during World War 2 and saw action during the Suez Crisis in 1956. It was last re-formed to support operations in the Falklands, flying off the decks of HMS HERMES and HMS INVINCIBLE.

At the end of 2020 the cost of the Lightning II jet was around £94m, down 24% on the original cost when the first aircraft were ordered at an individual cost of £124m.

US NAVY F-35B

What is the cowling right behind the cockpit used for?

The F-35B short takeoff and vertical landing (STOVL) capabilities are made possible through the Rolls-Royce patented shaft-driven LiftFan propulsion system installed behind the jet's cockpit, and an engine that can swivel 90 degrees when in short take-off/vertical landing mode. When the jet is set to 'Lift' mode two doors open behind the cockpit, one being the cowling for the air intake for the 50-inch titanium LiftFan. The cowling opens only when hovering, short take-offs, or landing vertically. It directs air down into the LiftFan and closes during normal flight covering the lift fan. The smaller doors behind the big cowling gives additional clean air to the engine which is operating high during this time.

CROWN COPYRIGHT/MOD

Leonardo Helicopters MERLIN HC3, HC3i, HC4

Role: Commando assault, load-lifting, troop movement
Engines: 3 x Rolls Royce/Turbomeca RTM 322 each developing 2,100 shp
Length: 74' 10" Rotor diameter: 61' Height: 21' 10"
Max. Weight: 32,120lb Max. Speed: 167 knots Crew: 1 or 2 pilots, 1 aircrewman
Avionics: Wescam MX-15 electro-optical/IR camera; defensive aids suite including directional IR countermeasures, AN/AAR-57 missile approach warning system, automatic chaff and flare dispensers
Armament: 1 x M3M 0.5" machine-gun in cabin door; 1 x 7.62mm machine-gun in cabin window

Squadron Service: 845, 846 Naval Air squadrons.

Notes: The first of 25 Merlin HC3s to be modified to HC4 standard was delivered by Leonardo Helicopters in 2017 and the last was due to be delivered in 2020, restoring an embarked capability to the Commando Helicopter Force, CHF. 7 aircraft have been modified to an interim HC3i standard to give some TAG capability until sufficient HC4s are available. The HC4 has a 'glass cockpit' similar to that of the HM2, power-folding main rotor head and tail pylon together with improved communications and defensive aids. Unlike the green HC3s, Merlin HC4s are painted grey. 845 NAS is eventually to have 10 aircraft deployable in up to 3 TAGs and 846 NAS is also to have 10 with an operational conversion/training flight, a maritime counter-terrorism flight and, after 2020, a TAG flight to back up 845. The remaining 5 airframes give deep maintenance flexibility and will act as attrition reserves.

The Merlin helicopter does not have the capability to lift and transport a jet engine for the F-35 which causes issues at the MoD. Due to funding constraints the MoD does not have a solution despite the Maritime Intra-theatre Lift Capability requiring the need to move people and equipment, especially parts for the F-35.

JOINT HELICOPTER COMMAND

Leonardo Helicopters WILDCAT AH1

Role: Battlefield reconnaissance; airborne command and control, force protection and troop transport.
Engines: 2 x LHTEC CTS 800-4N turboshafts each developing 1,362 shp
Length: 50' **Rotor diameter:** 42' **Height:** 12'
Max. Weight: 13,200lb **Max. Speed:** 157 knots **Crew:** 2 pilots & 1 gunner
Avionics: L-3 Wescam MX-15Di electro-optical/laser designator turret; digital mission planning system; Selex HIDAS 15 electronic warfare system
Armament: Door-mounted 0.5 inch M3M machine gun.

Squadron Service: 847 Naval Air Squadron, 1 Regiment Army Air Corps

Notes: 847 NAS is shore-based at RNAS Yeovilton and operates the Wildcat AH 1 as part of the Commando Helicopter Force, within the Joint Helicopter Command, to support 3 Commando Brigade with battlefield reconnaissance and airborne command and control of forces on the ground. 1 Regiment is also based at RNAS Yeovilton and operates, effectively, as a joint force with the RN Wildcat squadrons. It comprises a headquarters squadron plus 652, 659 and 661 Squadrons which operate their Wildcats as a specialised intelligence, surveillance and reconnaissance aircraft in support of troops on the ground. In the troop-lift role, Army Wildcats can lift up to 5 fully-equipped troops over short distances. Like 847 NAS they can be embarked to form part of a TAG when required and AAC pilots are trained to operate from the sea.

CROWN COPYRIGHT/MOD

Leonardo Helicopters APACHE AH1

Role: Attack and armed reconnaissance helicopter
Engines: 2 x Rolls Royce/Turbomeca RTM 322 turboshafts each developing 2,100 shp
Length: 58' 3" Rotor diameter: 48' Height: 15' 3"
Max. Weight: 15,075lb Max. Speed: 150 knots Crew: 2 pilots
Avionics: Selex HIDAS defensive aids suite; Longbow radar; optical and infrared target indication sensors.
Armament: Up to 16 AGM-114 Hellfire air-to-surface guided weapons; up to 4 Sidewinder air-to-air missiles; M230 30mm cannon with 1,160 rounds; up to 76 CRV-7 unguided air-to-surface missiles.

Squadron Service: 3 and 4 Regiments Army Air Corps

Notes: 3 Regiment AAC comprises 653, 662 and 663 Squadrons. 4 Regiment comprises 656 and 664 Squadrons and both formations are based at the AAC base at Wattisham and form part of the Joint Helicopter Command. Apaches of 656 Squadron flew successfully on operations over Libya with a TAG embarked in OCEAN during 2011 and at least one unit is maintained at high readiness for embarked operations as part of a TAG but in an emergency a larger number of Apaches could be embarked if required.

The Apache AH1 is to reach its out of service date in 2024 and be replaced by the Boeing AH-64D Apache Longbow attack helicopter.

Boeing CHINOOK HC4, HC4A and HC5

Role: Battlefield transport helicopter
Engines: 2 x Avco Lycoming T55-L-712 turboshafts each developing 3,750 shp
Length: 98' 9" Rotor diameter: 60' Height: 18' 8"
Max. weight: 50,000lb Max. speed: 160 knots Crew: 2 pilots & 2 aircrewmen/gunners
Avionics: Infrared jammer; missile warning system; integrated digital 'glass cockpit'; moving map tablet and improved crewman's work station.
Armament: up to 2 M 134 mini guns mounted in doorways; one M 60 machine gun on rear loading ramp.

Squadron Service: 7, 18, 27, 28(AC) Squadrons Royal Air Force

Notes: All 4 squadrons are based at RAF Odiham from where the 3 operational units can provide TAG detachments when required. The Chinook's rotor blades cannot fold but QUEEN ELIZABETH's side lifts are large enough to strike down the aircraft, fully spread, into the hangar and they can be embarked in significant numbers to support both amphibious military and humanitarian operations. Chinooks can carry 54 fully-equipped troops, 24 stretcher cases or loads up to 44,000lb carried both internally and externally over short distances. With extra fuel tanks they have a range of 1,000nm with a light load. Originally designed for the US Army, Chinooks are in widespread service throughout the world. The Boeing Chinook Helicopter entered service on the 22nd November 1980. Throughout its 40 years of service the Chinook has made an immeasurable contribution to the Service, supporting communities across the UK and operating in every major conflict since the Falklands War. Towards the end of 2020, the helicopter displayed the red, white and blue colours to celebrate it's 40th anniversary.

BAE Systems HAWK T2

Role: Advanced fast-jet training aircraft for RAF, RN and RM pilots
Engine: 1 x Rolls Royce Adour 951 FADEC/turbofan delivering 6,500lb of thrust
Length: 41' **Wingspan:** 32' 7" **Height:** 13' 1"
Max. Weight: 20,000lb **Max. Speed:** Mach 1 at altitude **Crew:** 1 or 2 pilots
Avionics: Two mission computers host simulations of sensor and weapons systems; a data link allows synthetic radar inputs for intercept training and synthetic electronic warfare threats. Inertial and GPS navigation systems.
Armament: 7 hardpoints capable of carrying a total of 6,800lb of weapons, including 1 x 30mm cannon pod on centreline, AIM-9 Sidewinder or ASRAAM missiles and bombs.

Squadron Service: 4(R) Squadron Royal Air Force

Notes: 4 (Reserve) Squadron forms part of Number 4 Flying Training School at RAF Valley within the Military Flying Training System and provides advanced fast-jet training for RAF, RN and RM pilots up to the standard required for conversion onto operational types. The Hawk T 2 has a 'glass cockpit' with 3 full-colour, multi-function displays, similar to those in the Typhoon and F-35B, which display navigation, weapons and system information intended to immerse student pilots into a complex, data-rich tactical flying environment from the outset rather than just learning to fly the aircraft.

Short TUCANO T1

Role: Basic fast-jet training aircraft for RAF, RN and RM pilots
Engine: 1 x Garrett TPE 331-12B turboprop delivering 1,100 shp
Length: 32' 4" Wingspan: 37' Height 11' 2"
Max. Weight: 7,220lb Max. Speed: 300 knots Crew: 1 or 2 pilots
Avionics: Standard communications fit
Armament: None

Squadron Service 72(R) Squadron Royal Air Force

Notes: Operated by 72 (Reserve) Squadron as part of Number 1 Flying Training School at RAF Linton-on-Ouse, an element of the Military Flying Training System, the Tucano provides basic training for student RAF, RN and RM fast-jet pilots and RAF weapons system operators; it handles like a jet aircraft but is significantly cheaper to operate. Plans to replace the Tucano with the Beechcraft T-6C Texan II in 2019 have been delayed.

Beech AVENGER T1

Role: Observer training
Engines: 2 x Pratt & Whitney PT6A-60A, each developing 1,050 shp
Length: 46' 8" Wingspan: 57' 11" Height: 14' 4"
Max. Weight: 15,000lb Max. Speed; 313 knots
Crew: 1 or 2 pilots, 4 student observers plus instructors
Avionics: Surface search and ground mapping radar
Armament: None

Squadron Service: 750 Naval Air Squadron

Notes: Avengers are civil-owned but military registered and used by 750 NAS at RNAS Culdrose as part of the MFTS. They provide Phase 3 training for RN observers and lead-in training for RAF AWACS systems operators. Phases 1 and 2 of the Observer Course are carried out by 703 Squadron at RAF Barkston Heath.

Airbus JUNO HT1

Role: Basic helicopter training
Engines: 2 x Turbomeca Arrius 2B, each developing 708 shp
Length: 39' 7" Rotor diameter: 33' 5" Height: 12' 4"
Max. Weight: 6,570lb Max. Speed: 140 knots
Crew: 2 pilots plus up to 6 passengers
Avionics: Defensive aids simulator; L-3 Wescam electro/optical camera
Armament: None

Squadron Service: 705 Squadron MFTS

Notes: The Juno HT1 began flying training at the Defence Helicopter School at RAF Shawbury in April 2018, replacing the Squirrel HT1. With twin engines and a night-vision goggle compatible glass cockpit, the new helicopter gives student pilots a better lead-in to operational types such as the Merlin and Wildcat than its predecessors. All 29 Junos are fitted with a defensive aids simulator operated by the instructor and wired for an electro/optical camera installation although at any one time only 10 will be so fitted with the aim of teaching students to operate, rather than just fly modern aircraft types.

CROWN COPYRIGHT/MOD

Eurocopter AS365N DAUPHIN 2

Role: Passenger movement and training support
Engines: 2 x Turbomeca Arriel 2C each developing 838 shp
Length: 39' 9" Rotor diameter: 39' 2" Height: 13' 4"
Max. Weight: 9,480lb Max. Speed: 155 knots Crew: 1 or 2 pilots plus up to 11 passengers
Avionics: None
Armament: None

Notes: Similar to the H-65 helicopters operated by the US Coast Guard, 2 of these civil-owned military-registered, COMR, helicopters are operated for the RN by Babcock Mission Critical Services Offshore Limited (known as Bond Offshore Helicopters until 25 April 2016) under contract. They are maintained at Newquay airport and used to support FOST in the sea areas off Plymouth. They are commonly tasked to transfer passengers between ships at sea but can also undertake a wide variety of other roles. On a day-to-day basis they fly from an operating facility within Devonport Naval base from which FOST staff can be flown from their headquarters directly to ships at sea.

Babcock operates a mixed fleet of helicopters on behalf of more than 10 major customers, specialising in providing offshore helicopter transportation services to North Sea and Irish Sea oil and gas platforms.

FLAG OFFICER SEA TRAINING COMMAND

Weapons of the Royal Navy

Sea Launched Missiles

Trident II D5

The American built Lockheed Martin Trident 2 (D5) submarine launched strategic missiles are Britain's only nuclear weapons and form the UK contribution to the NATO strategic deterrent. 16 missiles, each capable of carrying up to 6 UK manufactured thermonuclear warheads (but currently limited to 4 under current government policy), can be carried aboard each of the Vanguard-class SSBNs. Trident has a maximum range of 12,000 km and is powered by a three stage rocket motor. Launch weight is 60 tonnes, overall length and width are 13.4 metres and 2.1 metres respectively.

Tomahawk (BGM-109)

This is a land attack cruise missile with a range of 1600 km and can be launched from a variety of platforms including surface ships and submarines. Some 65 of the latter version were purchased from America to arm Trafalgar-class SSNs with the first being delivered to the Royal Navy for trials during 1998. Tomahawk is fired in a disposal container from the submarine's conventional torpedo tubes and is then accelerated to its subsonic cruising speed by a booster rocket motor before a lightweight F-107 turbojet takes over for the cruise. Its extremely accurate guidance system means that small targets can be hit with precision at maximum range, as was dramatically illustrated in the Gulf War and Afghanistan. Total weight of the submarine version, including its launch capsule is 1816 kg, it carries a 450 kg warhead, length is 6.4 metres and wingspan (fully extended) 2.54 m. Fitted in Astute & T-class submarines. It was announced in 2014 that the US Navy are to stop procuring the missile in 2015 which has implications for the production line, although an MoD spokesman expected this not to impact on UK requirements.

Harpoon

The Harpoon is a sophisticated surface-to-surface missile using a combination of inertial guidance and active radar homing to attack targets out to a range of 130 km, cruising at Mach 0.9 and carrying a 227 kg warhead. It is powered by a lightweight turbojet but is accelerated at launch by a booster rocket. Fitted to Type 23 frigates and four Type 45 destroyers. Harpoon was planned to be retired from Royal Navy service at the end of 2018, but this was extended to 2023. The future anti-ship missile system, a joint UK/French programme, will not be in service until 2030 at the very earliest.

Sea Viper (Aster 15/30)

Two versions of the Aster missile equip the Type 45 Destroyer, the shorter range Aster 15 and the longer range Aster 30. The missiles form the weapon component of the Principal Anti Air Missile System (PAAMS). Housed in a 48 cell Sylver Vertical Launch system, the missile mix can be loaded to match the ships requirement. Aster 15 has a range of 30 km while Aster 30 can achieve 100 km. The prime external difference between the two is the size of the booster rocket attached to the bottom of the missile. PAAMS is known as Sea Viper in RN service.

Sea Wolf

Short range rapid reaction anti-missile and anti-aircraft weapon. The complete weapon system, including radars and fire control computers, is entirely automatic in operation. Type 23 frigates carry 32 Vertical Launch Sea Wolf (VLS) in a silo on the foredeck. Basic missile data: weight 82 kg, length 1.9 m, wingspan 56 cm, range c.5-6 km, warhead 13.4 kg. The VLS missile is basically similar but has jettisonable tandem boost rocket motors. The Sea Wolf system is gradually being replaced by Sea Ceptor.

Sea Ceptor

Incorporating the Common Anti-Air Modular Missile (CAMM) family, being developed to replace the Rapier and Sea Wolf SAM systems, plus the ASRAAM short range Air-to-Air Missile. It will arm the Royal Navy's Type 23 frigates and its Type 26 Global Combat Ships. In Spring 2012 the MoD awarded MBDA UK a five-year Demonstration Phase contract worth £483 million to develop the missile for the RN. In September 2013 a £250 million contract was announced to manufacture the missile in the UK, sustaining around 250 jobs at MBDA sites in Stevenage, Filton and Lostock. Installation of the Sea Ceptor on Type 23 frigates started in 2015 with ARGYLL and the last will be completed by 2021. CAMM missiles will be fitted in the existing VL Sea Wolf silo (one canister per cell for a maximum of 32 missiles).

Guns

114mm Vickers Mk8 Mod 1

The Royal Navy's standard medium calibre general purpose gun which arms the Type 23 frigates and Type 45 destroyers. The Mod 1 is an electrically operated version of the original gun and is recognised by its angular turret. First introduced in 2001 it is now fitted in all Type 23 and Type 45 vessels. Rate of fire: 25 rounds/min. Range: 22,000 m. Weight of Shell: 21 kg.

Phalanx

A US-built CIWS designed around the Vulcan 20 mm rotary cannon. Rate of fire is 3000 rounds/min and effective range is c.1500 m. Fitted in Type 45 and some Wave, Bay and Fort Classes. Block 1B began entering service from 2009. Incorporates side mounted forward looking infra-red enabling CIWS to engage low aircraft and surface craft. In October 2012 it was announced that a further five Phalanx Block 1B mountings were to be procured to protect RFA ships.

DS30B 30mm

Single mounting carrying an Oerlikon 30mm gun. Fitted to Type 23 frigates and various patrol vessels and MCMVs. In August 2005 it was announced that the DS30B fitted in Type 23 frigates was to be upgraded to DS30M Mk 2 to include new direct-drive digital servos and the replacement of the earlier Oerlikon KCB cannon with the ATK Mk 44 Bushmaster II 30 mm gun. Consideration is already being given to purchasing additional DS30M Mk 2 systems for minor war vessels and auxiliaries.

GAM BO 20mm

A simple hand operated mounting carrying a single Oerlikon KAA 200 automatic cannon firing 1000 rounds/min. Maximum range is 2000 m. Carried by most of the fleet's major warships except the Type 23 frigates.

20mm Mk.7A

The design of this simple but reliable weapon dates back to World War II but it still provides a useful increase in firepower, particularly for auxiliary vessels and RFAs. Rate of fire 500-800 rounds/min.

Close Range Weapons

In addition to the major weapons systems, all RN ships carry a variety of smaller calibre weapons to provide protection against emerging terrorist threats in port and on the high seas such as small fast suicide craft. In addition it is sometimes preferable, during policing or stop and search operations to have a smaller calibre weapon available. Depending upon the operational environment ships may be seen armed with varying numbers of pedestal mounted General Purpose Machine Guns (GPMG). Another addition to the close in weapons is the Mk 44 Mini Gun, a total of 150 of which have been procured from the United States as a fleetwide fit. Fitted to a naval post mount, the Minigun is able to fire up to 3,000 rounds per minute, and is fully self-contained (operating off battery power).

Torpedoes

Sting Ray

A lightweight anti-submarine torpedo which can be launched from ships, helicopters or aircraft. In effect it is an undersea guided missile with a range of 11 km at 45 knots or 7.5 km at 60 knots. Length 2.1 m, diameter 330 mm. Type 23s have the Magazine Torpedo Launch System (MTLS) with internal launch tubes. Sting Ray Mod 1 is intended to prosecute the same threats as the original Sting Ray but with an enhanced capability against small conventionally powered submarines and an improved shallow-water performance.

Spearfish

Spearfish is a submarine-launched heavyweight torpedo which has replaced Tigerfish. Claimed by the manufacturers to be the world's fastest torpedo, capable of over 70 kts, its sophisticated guidance system includes an onboard acoustic processing suite and tactical computer backed up by a command and control wire link to the parent submarine. Over 20ft in length and weighing nearly two tonnes, Spearfish is fired from the standard 21-inch submarine torpedo tube and utilises an advanced bi-propellant gas turbine engine for higher performance. The Navy is investing £270m upgrading the Spearfish heavyweight torpedo by fitting a new warhead, a safer fuel system, an enhanced electronic brain and a fibre-optic guidance link with the parent submarine in order to improve accuracy and lethality. The warhead is at least six times more powerful than that carried by the Stringray lightweight torpedo. Enhanced Spearfish will be introduced to SSNs over the next three years and will be in service until the 2050s. Sea trials have recently been carried out with the frigate SUTHERLAND.

Future Weapons

Sea Venom

Formerly known as the Future Anti-Surface Guided Weapon (Heavy), Sea Venom is a high-subsonic 'drop-launch' missile in the 110 kg-class incorporating an imaging infrared seeker (with provisions for an additional semi-active laser guidance channel), a two-way datalink for operator-in-the-loop control, and a 30kg warhead. Designed by MBDA to replace the helicopter air-launched Exocet, the missile will have a range of up to 25 km and will be able to counter targets up to corvette size. The FASGW programme, comprising both Heavy and Light missiles, is a joint venture between the UK and France. The missile will equip the RNs Wildcat helicopter. In July 2014, AgustaWestland received a £90 million contract to integrate the respective variants for deployment from the Wildcat HMA2. Each aircraft will be able to carry four missiles and it is anticipated that Initial Operating Capability will be achieved in 2020.

Martlet

Formerly known as the Future Anti-Surface Guided Weapon (Light), this missile is designed to counter small boat and fast inshore attack craft threats. It is based on the laser beam-riding variant of the Thales Lightweight Multi-role Missile (LMM). With a range of up to 8 km it carries a 3 kg blast fragmentation/shaped charge warhead travelling at about Mach 1.5. Missiles will be carried in a five-round launcher (with each Wildcat able to carry up to four launchers). Alternatively a mix of two Sea Venom on the outer pylon and two five round Martlet on the inner weapons station can be carried. An active laser guidance unit integrated within the L-3 Wescam nose turret will support laser beam-riding guidance.

Future Cruise/Anti-ship Weapon

The UK and France have signed an agreement to explore future missile technologies with MBDA which covers a three-year concept phase to develop future long range weapons for the British and French Navies and Air Forces. Each country will contribute EUR50 million to this phase. The Future Cruise/Anti-Ship Weapon programme will look at options to replace and improve existing Naval and Air Force weapons systems in the next decade. The new generation missiles will be a successor to the Harpoon, SCALP and Storm Shadow. The FC/ASW (future cruise/anti-ship weapon) programme's aim is to have, by around 2030, a new generation of missiles.

At the end of the line...

MIKE BARCLAY

HMS Trenchant

Former HMS Diligence

Currently, the only RFA ship that appears on DESA's disposals list is the unique DILIGENCE. Known as the floating Swiss Army knife, RFA DILIGENCE was the RN's forward repair vessel, capable of acting as a floating repair base for all types of surface warships and, especially, for the maintenance of the RN's fleet of ballistic submarines. Despite the millions of £s that have been spent on the vessel's upkeep in recent years, around £44.5 million between 2007 and 2015, RFA DILIGENCE is getting on in years. The vessel has been laid up since 2015, first in Birkenhead, after completing a major refit at Cammell Laird, and latterly in Portsmouth Naval Base. There were reports last year that a commercial Dutch operator was interested in buying RFA DILIGENCE for continued service. However, this deal appears not to have progressed.

Since the previous edition the following vessels were sold, disposed of or are in long term storage and/or awaiting scrap:

PORTSMOUTH: ATHERSTONE; DILIGENCE; WALNEY; BRISTOL.

PLYMOUTH: TORBAY; TIRELESS; TRAFALGAR; TURBULENT; SCEPTRE; SUPERB; SPLENDID; SPARTAN; SOVEREIGN; CONQUEROR; VALIANT; WARSPITE.

ROSYTH: RESOLUTION; RENOWN; REPULSE; REVENGE; SWIFTSURE; CHURCHILL; DREADNOUGHT.

HMS Trenchant

Towards the end of March 2021 the Trafalgar-class nuclear-powered submarine HMS TRENCHANT sailed into her home port of Plymouth for the very last time. Devonport Naval Base welcomed home the oldest submarine in the Royal Navy fleet proudly flying her paying off pennant. As the submarine arrived at Plymouth Sound a number of her crew 'went up top' to line the casing. Serco tugs SD FAITHFUL and SD ADEPT sprayed a water salute over the submarine in recognition of her long and esteemed service in the Royal Navy. TRENCHANT was launched in 1986 by Vice Admiral Sir Arthur Hezlet - the commander of the original HMS TRENCHANT submarine during WW2. During her 35-years on patrol there have been many highlights of her service, two of which have been her ice-patrols. In 2016 the boat punched through the ice and emerged on the surface of the Arctic Ocean. This marked nearly a decade since a British boat had carried out this manoeuvre, re-generating the Submarine Service's under-ice capability. In 2018 in the harsh environment of the North Pole HMS TRENCHANT broke through the ice again in an exercise with the US Navy. She will be de-commissioned later in 2021.

Former HMS Bristol

In early February 2020, it was revealed that the Royal Navy would no longer use BRISTOL for training purposes with the announcement that the former Type 82 destroyer was not to have her life extended as a training ship. HMS BRISTOL is the second oldest Royal Navy warship in service after HMS VICTORY. She served for 57 years on the waters, both as a warship of the Royal Navy, serving the Falklands war; and as a training ship. BRISTOL (D23) was the only vessel of her class to be built for the Royal Navy. She was originally intended as the first of a class of large destroyers to escort the CVA-01 aircraft carriers projected to come into service in the early 1970s. Following the 1966 Strategic Defence Review the rest of the class were cancelled together with the CVA-01 carriers. In 1987 she was converted into a training ship and in October 2010 she was refitted at A&P Tyne. Facilities were brought in line with with health and safety standards. Other work included the removal of the redundant masts containing the ship's Type 1022 and Type 992Q search radars.

RBNS Al Zubarah

The former Falkland Islands patrol vessel HMS CLYDE has now swapped the cold waters of the South Atlantic for the much warmer ones of the Arabian Gulf, having been bought by the Kingdom of Bahrain for operation with the Royal Bahrain Naval Force (RBNF). No price has been revealed for the sale of the vessel. HMS CLYDE was handed over to the RBNF by BAE Systems Marine at a 'behind closed doors service' in Portsmouth Naval Base on 7 August 2020 and immediately commissioned as RBNS AL ZUBARAH. She is now the second largest warship in the RBNF, after the Oliver Hazard Perry-class frigate RBNS SABAH.

Former HMS Quorn

2020 witnessed the sale by DESA of the RN's youngest Hunt-class Mine Counter Measures Vessel (MCMV) QUORN, commissioned in1989, to the Lithuanian Navy for £2.5 million. The latter is a big fan of RN MCMVs, having acquired sister-ships HMS DULVERTON and HMS COTTESMORE in 2008. After major upgrading work in the UK, both vessels entered service in 2011 and operate as the Skalvis-class of MCMVs. The Lithuanian Navy wants QUORN to deliver the same capability as the Skalvis Class, meaning a significant upgrade programme will be required. It is hoped that she will be operational for her new owners by 2023.

Former HMS Atherstone

Also on the DESA's disposal list are two former Royal Navy Sandown-class MCMVs - ex HMS ATHERSTONE and ex HMS WALNEY, commissioned in 1986 and 1991 and decommissioned in 2017 and 2010 respectively. However, both vessel will not see further naval service as they have been stripped of almost all useable equipment and propulsion systems while laid-up in Portsmouth Naval Base and are up for sale for offers in excess of £30,000 each. DESA says that it is interested in "expressions of interest from parties who wish to be considered for this 'one-of-a-kind' proposed sale." DESA says both vessels are suitable for conversion and use as a houseboat, floating restaurant, floating bar, or even a floating office.

Former HMS Walney

ROBERT RADFORD

HMS Cavalier

> **❝** A National Audit Office report into the MoD's equipment plan 2019-2029 mentioned the defuelling and dismantling of redundant nuclear submarines. The MoD has deferred dismantling submarines on affordability grounds and has not disposed of any of the 20 redundant submarines it has decommissioned since 1980. The MoD has not defuelled a nuclear submarine since 2004. It now stores nine fuelled submarines. **❞**

At the end of the line ...

Readers may well find other warships afloat which are not mentioned in this book. The majority have fulfilled a long and useful life and are now relegated to non-seagoing duties. The following list gives details of their current duties:

Pennant No	Ship	Remarks
M29	BRECON	Hunt-class Minehunter - Attached to the New Entry Training Establishment, HMS RALEIGH, Torpoint, as a static Seamanship Training Ship.
M103	CROMER	Single Role Minehunter - Attached to BRNC, Dartmouth as a Static Training Ship.
L3505	SIR TRISTRAM	Refitted as a Static Range Vessel at Portland.
S50	COURAGEOUS	Nuclear-powered Submarine - On display at Devonport Naval Base. Can be visited during Base Tours.
C35	BELFAST (1938)	World War II Cruiser Museum ship - Port of London Open to the public daily.
D73	CAVALIER	World War II Destroyer & Oberon-class Submarine
S17	OCELOT	Museum Ships at Chatham. Open to the public.
S67	ALLIANCE	Submarine - Museum Ship at Gosport Open to the public daily.
LCT7074	LANDFALL	A D-Day veteran. Refloated in October 2014 six years after she sank at Birkenhead. After years of extensive restoration by NMRN at Portsmouth she has been moved to Southsea and is on display outside the D-Day Museum.
	BRITANNIA	Ex Royal Yacht at Leith. Open to the public.
	CAROLINE	Light Cruiser and veteran of the Battle of Jutland preserved at Belfast.
	M33	Coastal Monitor and veteran of the Gallipoli Campaign on display at Portsmouth as part of the National Museum of the Royal Navy.